Pride Before the FALL

Pride Before the FALL

The Trials of Bill Gates and the End of the Microsoft Era

JOHN HEILEMANN

HarperCollins*Publishers*

HarperCollins books may be purchased for educational, business, or sales promotional use. For information please write: Special Markets Department, HarperCollins Publishers, Inc., 10 East 53rd Street, New York, NY 10022.

FIRST EDITION

Designed by William Ruoto

Library of Congress Cataloging-in-Publication Data has been applied for.

ISBN 0-06-662117-8

01 02 03 04 05 ❖/RRD 10 9 8 7 6 5 4 3 2 1

For my mother, whom I miss.
For my father, whom I love.
And for Katrina Heron, who believed.

Pride goeth before destruction,
and a haughty spirit before a fall.

—PROVERBS 16:18

Contents

Prologue

THE
HUMBLING

THE JUDGE in Chicago wanted his signature. Just two little words on the bottom line: Bill. Gates.

It was early in March 2000, three full months after the formal, court-ordered mediation between Microsoft and the government had begun, and Bill Gates knew he hadn't much time. Any day now, federal judge Thomas Penfield Jackson would unveil his verdict in *United States v. Microsoft*, one of the largest, most consequential, and most controversial antitrust actions in American history. Nobody doubted what the outcome would be. The previous November, Jackson had disgorged a 207-page "findings of fact" that was searing in tone and staggering in the totality of its rejection of Microsoft's version of the events in question. If the

1

verdict fit the findings, it was going to be ugly—maybe ugly enough to bring about the dismemberment of the most valuable company on earth.

Microsoft's last hope for averting disaster lay in the hands of a different judge: the judge in Chicago, Richard A. Posner. The chief justice of the United States Court of Appeals for the Seventh Circuit, Posner was a conservative jurist with a towering reputation—a man described by the dean of the University of Chicago Law School as "the single greatest antitrust scholar and judge of this generation." Shortly after Judge Jackson had issued his findings of fact, he rang Judge Posner and implored him to step in as mediator between Microsoft and the Department of Justice (DOJ), whose relationship had degenerated during the lawsuit to a state of mutual contempt. Jackson wasn't sure if Posner would even take his call; so he was surprised and delighted when Posner accepted the invitation without batting an eye. For anyone else, trying to forge a peace between these two combatants would have been a fool's errand. But given Posner's exalted stature, Jackson hoped—prayed—he might just find a way to pull it off.

Posner kept his chambers on the 27th floor of the Everett M. Dirksen federal courthouse in downtown Chicago. Every week since the end of November, he had summoned a team of lawyers and economists from the DOJ and a similar team from Microsoft, always meeting the two sides separately, never letting them in the same room together. In the first two months of the mediation, according to one participant, Posner in effect "retried the case"— rehearsing the arguments, reviewing the evidence. Posner's dedication and thoroughness impressed Gates mightily. In January, Microsoft's chairman flew out from Seattle for a face-to-face session with the judge; afterward, they spoke by phone on nearly a dozen occasions, delving in extraordinary depth into the details of Microsoft's business. "The guy's super-smart," Gates told me later, bestowing on Posner his highest plaudit.

By February, Posner felt comfortable enough with the business issues to start trying to hammer out a settlement. (His grasp of the technology was shakier; even after weeks of tutoring, the concept of a "default Web browser" still baffled him.) Posner's method of seeking common ground was to draft a series of proposed consent decrees that would place certain limits on Microsoft's conduct. After presenting each draft to the opposing parties, Posner solicited their comments and criticisms, then cranked out another draft to push the ball forward. For a month or so, it went on like this, back and forth, to and fro, round and round—until they arrived at Draft 14. With Draft 14, Posner thought he'd come close to crafting a settlement that was tough enough to satisfy the DOJ but not so tough that Microsoft would recoil. When the *t*'s were crossed and the *i*'s dotted, Posner asked Gates if he could live with Draft 14. When Gates said that he could, Posner told him he wanted to demonstrate emphatically to the DOJ that Microsoft was serious—and the best way to do that would be for Gates to put his name to the proposal.

At Microsoft there were many who thought Posner naive. The government would never be satisfied, even if the firm were to sacrifice its firstborn—or, something rather more precious, its source code. Others simply thought Draft 14 too draconian. But although Gates saw the skeptics' points, he was anxious to put this whole nightmare behind him. He swallowed hard and scrawled his signature.

The skeptics were right: it wasn't enough. The DOJ wanted more restrictions on Microsoft's behavior, and fewer loopholes, than Draft 14 contained. Yet Posner still believed that a settlement could happen. For another month, he kept churning out drafts—

Draft 15, Draft 16, Draft 17. In the last week in March, Posner called Judge Jackson and asked for 10 days more; he was near, very near, to securing a deal. (So confident was Jackson that Posner would succeed, he took off on vacation for San Francisco.) By March 29, Draft 18 was complete. It reflected the DOJ's final offer.

In Gates's office in Redmond, Washington, the chairman's inner circle convened for one of the company's most fateful debates. Throughout the mediation, Gates had relied for advice on a handful of people: Microsoft's newly elevated CEO, Steve Ballmer; its general counsel, William Neukom; the senior executives Paul Maritz, James Allchin, and Robert Muglia. The document before them required that Microsoft set a uniform price list for Windows, barred it from striking exclusive contracts with Internet service and content providers, and forced it to open its application programming interfaces (APIs), the software hooks that allow programs to run on top of an operating system. And although Draft 18 would let Microsoft add new features to Windows—features such as Web browsing, which had spurred this lawsuit in the first place—PC manufacturers were granted the right to demand versions of the operating system without those features; and also the right to license the Windows source code, so that they could modify the computer desktop, integrate rival software, or add features of their own choosing.

There was no shortage of critics who would say this was all trivial tinkering, modest stuff of marginal utility. But the Microsoft high command didn't see it that way. Even for those executives who had been asked by Gates to play the devil's advocate in favor of settlement—Maritz and Muglia—Draft 18 was a bridge too far. It was not a proposal that Gates could sign on to.

In Silicon Valley and in Washington, DC, Gates's decision to reject Draft 18 was viewed as the crowning blunder in a succession of blunders that had marked his three-year battle with the federal government. It was an act of bloody-mindedness, of myopia, of hubris. Yet in the weeks and months that followed his refusal to settle, Gates never displayed the slightest hint of doubt about the decision he'd made and the offer he'd spurned. The son of a lawyer, steeped in the language of contracts, Gates believed that he knew a bad deal when he saw one; and that Draft 18 was a deal which would have wrecked his business. He was also aware that the courts were imperfect, and he considered Judge Jackson's more imperfect than most. But Gates had "faith," he told me, "that in the final analysis, the judicial system will come up with absolutely the right answer."

Whatever the logic of Gates's gamble, its immediate effect was swift and irrevocable. On March 31, Microsoft's Bill Neukom sent material to Judge Posner that would form the basis of Draft 19, which Posner then read by phone to the DOJ. The very next afternoon, April 1, still four days shy of his self-imposed deadline, the mediator declared his mediation a failure.

In public, and even more pointedly in private, Microsoft blamed the breakdown on the coalition of state attorneys general who had been the DOJ's partners in prosecution since the beginning of the case. In the crazy final days of the negotiations, the states had sent Posner a laundry list of demands considerably in excess of the DOJ's. In his only public utterance about the mediation—a written statement issued the day he called his efforts to a halt—Posner was studiously ambiguous about the precise cause of the collapse. Citing only "differences among the parties," he praised the professionalism of Microsoft and the DOJ, but made no mention of the attorneys general—an omission that seemed to many observers freighted with meaning. However, in an early version of his statement, which Posner shared with only a few people, the judge had gone out of his way to rap the states on the knuckles for their left-field intercession, while at the same time indicating that the truly insurmountable gap was "between" Microsoft and the DOJ.

With the mediation kaput, Judge Jackson hustled back from the coast and delivered his verdict on April 3. It was nearly as gruesome as expected. A month later, the DOJ and the states asked that the court split Microsoft into two companies: one containing its operating-system business, the other containing its application-software and Internet businesses. On June 7, Jackson agreed, ordering exactly the breakup the government requested.

It was the spring in Redmond when illusions were shattered, when old verities crumbled and the stock price tumbled, when everything that was solid melted into the air. By the time Jackson handed down his breakup order, Microsoft's value on the Nasdaq stock exchange had been chopped nearly in half since March, wiping out more than $200 billion in wealth. Competitors crowed. The press piled on. Private class-action antitrust lawyers began to swarm. In late June, Microsoft unveiled with great fanfare its grand new Internet strategy, and an industry that for so long had hung on its every hiccup, that had trembled at the sound of its virtual footsteps, dismissed the initiative as half-cooked vaporware— or, more charitably, yawned. Three months later, a yearlong exodus of talent reached its peak when Paul Maritz, the most powerful executive at Microsoft after Gates and Ballmer, announced he was leaving. Even for the truest of true believers, it seemed, faith had become a scarce commodity.

THE HUMBLING of Microsoft was the last great business story of the 20th century and the first great riddle of the 21st. There are fancier ways of putting it, but the riddle was this: How did it happen?

Perhaps no corporation in history had ever risen so far so fast. Having celebrated its 25th anniversary in 2000, Microsoft was no longer a fresh-faced child or even a gangly adolescent: adulthood was upon it. Yet among the totemic firms of the past century, from Standard Oil and US Steel to General Motors and General Electric, none had attained such stature, power, or profitability in so breathtakingly short a time. Even within the computer industry, where awareness of Microsoft's ascent had always been acute, people often forgot just how quickly it had happened. As recently as 1992 or 1993, the company, though plenty influential, was by no means seen as some omnipotent leviathan. Five years later, that had changed. In the autumn of 1997, when the Justice Department first took after Microsoft in a serious way, Gates's many rivals in Silicon Valley applauded. But their pleasure was tempered by a daunting perception that Microsoft was so indomitable, and the government so "dynamically anticlueful," as one digital quip-merchant put it, that nothing much would come of the DOJ's pursuit.

Theories abounded as to why things turned out so spectacularly otherwise. Some observers maintained that the outcome was more or less inevitable; that Microsoft's business practices, once brought to light, would have been enough to convict it in any court in the land. As a DOJ lawyer once said to me, "It was the stuff they did before the case was even filed that sealed their fate." Others suggested that Microsoft's history was bound to catch up with it from another direction; that its enemies in the Valley had been lying in wait, ready to strike at the first sign of weakness. (Not surprisingly, this was a theory that found favor with Gates.) Still others dwelled on Microsoft's tactical errors—on the ineptitude of its lawyers and its incompetence in the realm of high politics. And still others focused on Gates himself; on his arrogance, and on the insularity and isolation of the culture he'd wrought.

There were kernels of truth in each of these theories, but even taken together they fell short of eureka. What they failed to capture was the sometimes random confluence of forces at work: the way people with disparate agendas and mixed motives came crashing together to produce an outcome that seemed obvious only in retrospect.

All through its conduct, the Microsoft trial was compared to a war. "The War of the Roses," said Judge Jackson, or "the fall of the House of Tudor. Something medieval." But war is hell not simply because it's so bloody. War is hell because it's so unpredictable, so chaotic, so hot and dusty and shot through with confusion. The Microsoft trial was a war that neither side actually wanted to fight, in which unexpected alliances arose and old enmities surfaced at the most inopportune moments. It was war in which one hand rarely knew what the other was doing and carefully planned offensive ganged aft agley. Coincidence, timing, and blind shithouse luck all played their parts. And so did large acts of cowardice and small acts of courage, often committed by unknown soldiers.

This is the story of the generals in that war, of Bill Gates and Bill Neukom, Joel Klein and David Boies. But it is also the story of those unknown soldiers—people you've never heard of, whose tales have never been told. It's the story of Susan Creighton, the sweet-tempered antitrust lawyer who was Netscape's secret weapon. It's the story of Mark Tobey, the Texan crusader who took up the case when the Feds were still sleeping. It's the story of Mike Hirshland, the Republican Senate aide who found in Microsoft an unlikely passion, and it's the story of Dan Rubinfeld, the economist whose theories helped push the DOJ where it was hesitant to go. It's the story of Steve McGeady, the Intel apostate who took the stand against Gates. And it's the story of Mike Morris, the lawyer from Sun Microsystems who mounted a lobbying campaign that brought together some of Microsoft's most powerful opponents, and that was one of Silicon Valley's most closely guarded secrets—until now.

Acting sometimes in concert and sometimes alone, these unheralded characters and others like them accomplished things long regarded as impossible. They thrust Silicon Valley neck-deep into the swamps of Washington, DC. They put the high-tech industry's dirty laundry on display for all to see. They made antitrust law into national news. And they felled a giant that had once seemed invincible.

This is the story of the end of an era—and also of more than one kind of innocence.

Chapter 1

THE CASE THAT ALMOST WASN'T

THOUGH NO ONE at the company knew it at the time, Microsoft's troubles with the Department of Justice began in earnest in the spring of 1996, with the literary aspirations of two amateur authors in Silicon Valley. Since 1990, when the Federal Trade Commission (FTC) opened the first government probe into the firm's practices, Microsoft had been under the antitrust microscope more or less constantly; not a year had passed without it receiving at least one civil investigative demand (CID) for documents. As one federal inquiry morphed into the next, Gates and Ballmer gradually came to view the investigations not merely as legal scrutiny but as a kind of proxy warfare (and, later, as nothing less than a vast high-tech conspiracy) instigated by their enemies in the Valley and elsewhere. Yet as suspicious as they were about the source of their regulatory entanglements, Microsoft's leaders could scarcely have dreamed that so much damage would be unleashed by a quiet woman who called herself a "law-and-order Republican," a shrill man who was regarded by some as mildly unhinged, and the book they wrote together—a book that was never published in any form, and whose contents would long remain shrouded in secrecy.

Susan Creighton and Gary Reback were not, however, your typical wannabe wordsmiths. They were lawyers and antitrust specialists with Silicon Valley's preeminent law firm, Wilson Sonsini Goodrich & Rosati. They were passionate, smart, articulate, and angry. They had been retained by Netscape to tell the world, not to mention the DOJ, about the myriad ways in which Microsoft was endeavoring to drive the pioneering start-up six feet under. And they were rapidly approaching the end of their rope.

It was Reback who served as the duo's frontman. Throughout the computer business and the government, he was known as a guy who got paid to complain about Gates—the rough Silicon Valley equivalent of drawing a salary for breathing. Over the years, Reback had amassed a client roster that included some of the industry's most prominent firms—from Apple and Sun to Borland and Novell, though not all of them admitted it—and had earned a reputation as Redmond's most relentless and strident critic. The cover of *Wired* in August 1997 declared him "Bill Gates's Worst Nightmare."

Nightmarish or not, he was a piece of work. A Tennessee-born Jew in his late forties, Reback wore sharp suits, wire-rimmed glasses, and a perpetually pained expression. When he talked about Microsoft—which was pretty much constantly—his demeanor was fretfulness punctuated with blind outrage. His voice teetered on the edge of whine. "The only thing J. D. Rocke-feller did that Bill Gates hasn't done," Reback would wail, "is use dynamite against his competitors!" Crusader and showboat, ego-tist and quote machine, he had a taste for avant-garde economic theories and a tendency to level extravagant accusations without much hard proof to back them up. He was, in the strictest sense, a zealot: a man both fanatical and fanatically earnest in his beliefs. Later, when the DOJ decided to go after Microsoft, a government lawyer was assigned to "deal" with Reback. "His heart's in the right place," this lawyer said. "But he's twisted. He leaves me these voice-mails in the middle of the night, raving about all kinds of stuff. He really needs some help." History might well have judged Reback a marginal figure, just another Gates-hating ranter, were it not for one inconvenient fact: almost everything he claimed turned out to be true.

In Reback, Microsoft faced an adversary with a rare combina-tion of technical savvy and antitrust expertise. As an undergrad at Yale, he had worked his way through school by programming com-puters for the economics department; as a law student at Stanford, he had studied antitrust under the late William Baxter, who, as the head of the DOJ's antitrust division under Ronald Reagan, would oversee the breakup of AT&T. Susan Creighton recalled, "Gary liked to tell the story of how Baxter once said, 'We want companies to succeed, and when they succeed so well that they become monopolies, we should give them a tickertape parade down Wall Street—and then break them up.' I don't know if Baxter actually said that, and if he did say it whether he meant it literally, but Gary thought it sounded pretty good."

Reback's history with Microsoft was long, tangled, and not without its ironies. In the early 1980s, he secured for Apple the copyright registration for the Macintosh graphical user interface, a copyright over which Apple would eventually wage a nasty and protracted lawsuit with Microsoft. Not long afterward, a bearded, elfin entrepreneur from Berkeley appeared on Reback's doorstep and asked for help in selling his fledgling software company. The company was called Dynamical Systems Research; the entrepreneur, Nathan Myhrvold. After Apple passed up the deal, Microsoft stepped in, buying Myhrvold's start-up and Myhrvold along with it for $1.5 million. Forever after, Reback would be convinced that this transaction had been pivotal to the rise of Windows, in which Myhrvold played a key role. It was a conclusion that filled Reback with no end of guilt.

The lawyer became an anti-Microsoft missionary. As first the FTC and then the DOJ looked into the company, Reback peppered the Feds with briefs alleging a litany of predatory sins. In July 1994, the DOJ sued Microsoft for violating the Sherman Antitrust Act, only to drop the suit shortly thereafter and enter into a consent decree with the company. The agreement contained only a few mild curbs on Microsoft's behavior; Gates himself summarized its effect bluntly: "nothing." At the behest of a clutch of Microsoft's rivals in the Valley, who saw the decree as a Potemkin remedy, Reback spearheaded a spirited, but ultimately futile, campaign in federal court to scuttle it.

Indeed, all of Reback's warnings went unheeded, with one exception. That fall, Microsoft announced a plan to take over the financial-software firm Intuit for $1.5 billion. Reback, working primarily on behalf of an anonymous client (it was, in fact, the database company Sybase), prepared a white paper on the deal for the DOJ. Replete with novel economic concepts such as "network effects" and "increasing returns," the paper argued that if the merger wasn't stopped, Microsoft would come to rule online financial services just as it had the PC desktop. Reback was warned by the DOJ's chief economist that his analysis might be rejected as "totally preposterous." But it wasn't. In April 1995, the government moved to block the Intuit deal, and, rather than wage a costly battle, Microsoft bailed.

The victory was sweet for Reback, but all too fleeting. Two months later, on June 21, he received a call from a longstanding Wilson Sonsini client, Jim Clark. Clark was a well-known figure in Silicon Valley, a former Stanford professor who in the early 1980s had founded the 3-D workstation powerhouse Silicon Graphics. In 1994, Clark left SGI and teamed up with Marc Andreessen, the technical wunderkind who as an undergrad had led the team of student hackers that developed the first graphical Web browser, to found Netscape Communications. By the middle of 1995, Netscape's Navigator browser was the world's most rapidly proliferating piece of software and Netscape was the Valley's hottest start-up, one that was attracting attention throughout the industry—not least from Redmond.

Earlier that June day, Clark told Reback, a team of Microsoft engineers and executives had visited Netscape's headquarters in Mountain View, met with its CEO, Jim Barksdale, its marketing chief, Mike Homer, and Andreessen, and offered them a "special relationship." If Netscape would abandon much of the browser market to Microsoft, if it would agree not to compete with Microsoft in other areas, if it would allow Microsoft to invest in Netscape and have a seat on its board of directors, everything between the two companies would be wine and roses. If not . . .

"They basically said, OK, we have this nice shit sandwich for you," Mike Homer said later. "You can put a little mustard on it if you want. You can put a little ketchup on it. But you're going to eat the fucking thing or we're going to put you out of business."

The next day, Reback phoned Joel Klein, the former deputy White House counsel who had recently been named the second-ranking lawyer in the antitrust division, and persuaded him to send Netscape a CID for some detailed notes Andreessen had taken during the meeting. A few weeks later, Reback flew out to Washington with Clark, Andreessen, and Homer to state their case in person. The DOJ lawyers listened politely, jotted a few things down, said thanks—and then promptly forgot about it.

Thus began a pattern that would repeat itself again and again over the next two years. By the following spring, Barksdale & Co. were hearing a stream of reports about Microsoft's efforts to "cut off Netscape's air supply"—a phrase that would later acquire talismanic status—not least that Microsoft had threatened to cancel Compaq Computer's Windows license when Compaq tried to replace Microsoft's browser, Internet Explorer, with Netscape Navigator on some of its machines. With the browser war turning vicious and Netscape's complaints to the government getting nowhere, Reback and the company's general counsel, Roberta Katz, decided that desperate measures were in order. They would put Netscape's story down on paper, find a publisher, and present their plight in the bookstores of America.

The task of penning this opus would fall to Reback's colleague, Susan Creighton. Cerebral and literary where Reback was blustery and verbal, Creighton was a Harvard- and Stanford-educated attorney who had clerked on the Supreme Court for Justice Sandra Day O'Connor. She was every bit Reback's intellectual equal, and, they both agreed, the far better writer of the two. On May 1, therefore, Creighton sat down at her desk at home, surrounded by reams of documents, her infant child perched on her lap, and began tapping away.

Three months later, Creighton emerged with a 222-page piece of anti-Microsoft agitprop (including charts and tables courtesy of her husband, a local professor and desktop-publishing enthusiast). The tome would eventually bear the dust-dry title "White Paper Regarding Recent Anticompetitive Conduct of Microsoft Corporation," but its substance was anything but arid. Explicitly written for a broader audience than lawyers and techies, Creighton's book read less like a legal treatise than a true-crime potboiler, a high-tech *Executioner's Song*. Creighton spun the tale of Microsoft's 20-year rise to power; of how it had employed a blend of strategic brilliance and nefarious tactics to destroy its competitors and hence "to acquire virtually complete control over what is arguably the most important tool in the American work-place"; and of how, faced with a potent new challenger, it had "engaged in a variety of anticompetitive acts that surpass its previous illegal conduct."

Chief among those acts was what Creighton characterized as a naked attempt to divide the browser market at the meeting with Netscape the previous June. The white paper alleged that Microsoft had been withholding APIs that Netscape needed for its browser to plug into Windows 95, which was due to be released a few months later. "If we had a special relationship, you wouldn't be in this position," one of the men from Redmond had said, according to Andreessen's notes. The Microsoft people made clear that their company planned to build a browser for Windows 95, but also that they had limited interest in doing the same for the Macintosh, or for the Unix operating system, or even for older versions of Microsoft's OS, like Windows 3.0 and 3.1. "Would you be interested in having a partnership where NS gets all the non-Win95 stuff and MS gets all the Win95 stuff?" Andreessen's notes described a Microsoft executive as saying. "If NS doesn't want to, that's one thing. If NS does want to, then we can have our special relationship."

When Netscape spurned Microsoft's offer of collusion, Creighton wrote, Gates's firm had used its muscle with Internet service providers (ISPs) and original equipment manufacturers (OEMs)—as PC manufacturers are known—to shut down Netscape's distribution channels. The white paper accused Microsoft of illegally tying its browser to Windows. And of predatory pricing. And of exclusive dealing. And even of offering "secret side payments potentially amounting to *hundreds of millions* of dollars" to distributors to keep Netscape software off their customers' desktops. The evidence for these claims was sometimes thin, and based almost completely on hearsay. (Given the fact that Creighton did not have subpoena power, that was unavoidable.) But the claims were colorful, incendiary, and entirely plausible.

Equally plausible, if equally controversial, was Creighton's hypothesis as to Microsoft's motives. With help from Reback and Garth Saloner, a leading-edge Stanford economist who had assisted in drafting the Intuit white paper, Creighton put forward a nuanced theory of "monopoly maintenance": that Microsoft's primary objective was not to dominate the browser market for its own sake, but rather to protect its dominance over operating systems. What Gates realized, Creighton argued, was that the browser was more than just another software application—it was potentially a rival platform that held out the possibility of turning Windows into a commodity, and, as Gates himself put it, an "all but irrelevant" commodity at that.

"This is, at bottom, a very simple case," the white paper concluded. "It is about a monopolist (Microsoft) that has maintained its monopoly (desktop operating systems) for more than ten years. That monopoly is threatened by the introduction of a new technology (Web software) that is a partial substitute—and, in time, could become a complete substitute—for the monopoly product. Before that can happen, the monopolist decides to eliminate its principal rival (Netscape), and thereby protect its continued ability to receive monopoly rents. The monopolist is aided by the fact that circumstances are ideal for its predatory strategy: The monopolist has vast resources, while its rival has very modest ones; barriers to entry are high; and, once the rival is out of the way, the monopolist's road ahead looks clear."

THE IMPLICATIONS of the white paper were stark and chilling—perhaps too chilling. For when Creighton and Reback delivered the finished document to Netscape, the reaction was unexpectedly schizophrenic. On one hand, Creighton remembered, "Barksdale and the others said to us, 'Thank you! Someone has finally put into words what we've been trying to say; it's like we've found our voice.'" Yet the white paper made painfully clear how dire Netscape's predicament was. "As people at the company saw what their position looked like in black and white, there was increasing concern about making it public," Creighton said. "They said, 'Jeez, there's no way we can let this get out.'" In particular, Barksdale was worried about the reaction of Wall Street. "My fear was that people would read it as the whinings of some sad-sack loser," he recalled. "What would the markets think if we said, 'If the government doesn't help us, we're doomed'?"

And so it was determined that, rather than aiming for an audience of thousands, the Netscape white paper would have an audience of one: the DOJ. Creighton was crestfallen; Reback, enraged. Not only had the DOJ already demonstrated its lack of interest in Netscape's ongoing evisceration, but now Joel Klein had been named the acting head of the antitrust division.

Reback had no love for Klein, whose first major victory at the DOJ had come in 1995 when he defended the government's consent decree with Microsoft against Reback's challenge in federal court. Reback's suspicions, along with those of many in the Valley, only deepened when soon thereafter Klein took the lead in deciding that the DOJ would do nothing to halt Microsoft's plan to put an icon for its fledging online service, the Microsoft Network, on the Windows 95 desktop. A few months later, when the two men appeared together on an antitrust panel at the Harvard Law School, a fight broke out between them, during which Reback lambasted the DOJ as being full of "Microsoft's running dogs." At a dinner later that evening at the Harvard Faculty Club, Klein surprised even those at the table less adamant than Reback with his reluctance to pursue the company. "What if we hurt them and in the process we hurt the economy?" Klein asked. On returning to California, Reback told Creighton, "Joel doesn't get it. He's just fucking hopeless."

For one brief moment, Reback's pessimism seemed mistaken. In September 1996, not long after the Netscape white paper was shipped off to Washington, the DOJ announced it was opening an investigation into Microsoft's Internet activities. Years later, after their triumph in court, Klein and his allies would point to this as evidence that, as soon as Netscape came forward with credible allegations, the DOJ had jumped on the case like a dog on a bone. But this was revisionist history on a massive scale. The DOJ's investigative team consisted of a couple of lawyers working part-time in the San Francisco field office. In the course of the next year—a year in which, for all practical purposes, Netscape was reduced to rubble—those DOJ lawyers sent Microsoft a single CID, limited in scope to the company's dealings with Internet access providers, and a single CID to Netscape. There were no interviews, no depositions, no phones ringing off the hook. And when Reback or Creighton talked to the DOJ's lawyers, the conversations were marked by "a complete lack of meaningful engagement," Creighton said. "It was like, 'We're the police and you're taxpayers, so we have to listen to you complain. But don't expect us to do anything anytime this century." Reback recalled, "One of them actually said to me, 'browser, schmowser.' "

Up in Redmond, the impression of the Justice Department's interest in the case was much the same. In the spring of 1997, Bill Neukom received a call from Phil Malone, the DOJ lawyer who was heading up the Microsoft investigation out of the San Francisco office. Malone informed Neukom that the government wasn't planning to challenge the company's recently announced acquisition of a Silicon Valley start-up called WebTV. "Then Malone says, 'It doesn't look like this browser thing is going anywhere,' " another Microsoft lawyer recalled. "A little while later, we got another signal from him that it would all be over pretty quickly. We were popping champagne corks up here."

The bubbly turned out to be somewhat premature. Down in the Valley, Reback and Creighton, insanely frustrated though they were, had yet to concede defeat. If Klein wouldn't act of his own volition, they would simply have to goad him, or bait him, or shame him into doing it. The Netscape lawyers began lobbying anyone willing to lend them an ear. The FTC. The Senate Judiciary Committee. The European Commission. They drafted new white papers, these less confidential. And they trawled for allies among companies outside Silicon Valley—American Airlines, Walt Disney, publishers, banks—that might one day find themselves reliant on, or beholden to, Microsoft.

The most promising nibble came from an unlikely pond: the office of the Texas Attorney General. Reback, of course, knew that Texas was home to a thriving high-tech economy, and to two of the world's biggest PC OEMs, Compaq and Dell. But he wasn't aware that it was also home to a populist, reformist assistant attorney general named Mark Tobey, who'd become suspicious of Gates's power after reading a story in *Time* magazine about the browser wars. Within weeks of examining the original white paper, Tobey issued a set of CIDs to Microsoft and Netscape. When the documents arrived, he was fast persuaded that the case was worth pursuing. From then on, Tobey became Reback's staunchest ally in lobbying his peers in the offices of other state attorneys general around the country to look into Microsoft's behavior.

At first, the state AGs were more than reluctant, but as the summer of 1997 unfolded, Microsoft seemed intent on providing them with ample reasons to change their minds. First there was an article in *The Wall Street Journal* in which Reback's old friend Nathan Myhrvold was quoted as saying that Microsoft's strategy for Internet commerce was to get a "vig" (short for "vigorish," bookmakers' slang for a cut of the action) from every transaction on the Net that used Microsoft technology— every transaction on the Net, that is. Then came stories that Microsoft was negotiating a similar arrangement with cable-television firms when it came to digital TV. There was also Microsoft's high-profile, $150 million investment in Apple, a deal which marked the official end of what was once computing's fiercest rivalry, demonstrated that Steve Jobs's company was dependent on Bill Gates's for its very survival, and was seen in the Valley as a mortal blow to Netscape, whose browser was being ousted from its last refuge, the Mac desktop. Suddenly, in state AGs' offices and on Capitol Hill, people began to wonder if Microsoft really was the new Standard Oil. And, just as suddenly, Reback found that his alarmist alarums were being met with the most welcome three words an agitator can hear: "Tell us more."

His campaign finally starting to catch sparks, Reback planned to ignite a conflagration. After submitting to the DOJ another Netscape white paper—in which he and Creighton contended that Microsoft's goal was to gain a chokehold over all of online commerce—he quickly orchestrated a series of secret meetings with many of the allies he'd managed to round up, arranging for the DOJ's Phil Malone to witness the proceedings. "I had tried to start a fire with flint, I had tried to start a fire with a magnifying glass, I had done everything I could to start this fire, but I was still being ignored," Reback said. "I had to create an event that couldn't be ignored."

For two solid days in the last week of August, Reback turned Wilson Sonsini's Palo Alto offices into a kind of anti-Microsoft three-ring circus. In one conference room, lawyers on the staff of the Senate Judiciary Committee's chairman, Utah Republican Orrin Hatch, huddled with an assortment of Silicon Valley executives, collecting leads and gathering evidence of Microsoft's alleged malfeasance. In another conference room down the hall, the general counsels to a number of Microsoft's competitors, including Netscape, Sun, and Sabre—the airline industry's computerized reservation system, which Microsoft planned to take on with its travel site Expedia.com—held brainstorming sessions to map out a wide-ranging political campaign against Redmond on Capitol Hill, in the statehouses, and in the press. The meeting would prove to be the birth of ProComp, the leading anti-Microsoft lobbying outfit in Washington, DC.

But the center ring was in the law firm's main conference room, where Mark Tobey, seated beside Malone, Reback, Creighton, Netscape's Roberta Katz, and representatives from the AG's offices of several other states, conducted the first-ever depositions in what would become *US v. Microsoft*. There, Marc Andreessen,

Mike Homer, and other top Netscape executives laid out detailed accounts of many of the incidents in the white papers, including, most important, the June 1995 meeting at which Microsoft had allegedly made its proposal to carve up the browser market with Netscape. When Tobey asked Andreessen why he had taken notes on the meeting, the tyro replied, "I thought it might be a topic of discussion at some point with the US government on antitrust issues." (During the trial, Microsoft would cite this comment as evidence that the meeting was a setup, while Netscape and the DOJ would retort that Andreessen was just being sarcastic. "Bull-shit, on both counts," Andreessen said later. "I'd read all the books. I knew their MO. We were a little start-up. They were Microsoft, coming to town. I thought, Uh-oh. I know what happens now.")

As the depositions went on, Malone sat silently and took it all in. For the past year, he had been in charge of the DOJ's desultory inquiry; now, incredibly, he was watching as a state-level law-enforcement official—from Texas, no less—seized the initiative in an investigation of what was then the world's second most valuable corporation. Reback was taunting him mercilessly: "Phil, whaddaya think? That didn't sound like a market-division proposal, now did it?" But Malone somehow managed not to lose his composure. Until the very end, that is.

"When the depositions were over," Reback recalled, "Tobey goes up to Malone and says, 'This looks like the endgame. The only remedy I can see is to break Microsoft up.' And Malone turned purple. Purple! Here the DOJ isn't doing anything, and Tobey is saying, Hey guys, it's over. I really thought that Phil was about to have a coronary."

For Reback and Creighton, the August meetings at Wilson Sonsini marked a turning point. The lawyers from the Senate Judiciary Committee were leaning their way, and had started talking about the possibility of holding hearings on competition (or the lack thereof) in the software industry—and even, perhaps, of summoning Gates himself to Capitol Hill. Tobey and the states, a contingent that had grown to include Massachusetts and New York, were in hot pursuit. With the founding of ProComp, Microsoft's congenitally disorganized competitors seemed for once to be getting their act together. And, through the good offices of a shaken Phil Malone, the Netscape attorneys had fired a loud, bracing shot across the DOJ's bow.

The message was clear: the Microsoft matter wasn't going away. Yet the real question remained unanswered: was Joel Klein finally ready to listen?

Chapter 2

THE ACCIDENTAL TRUSTBUSTER

MIKE HIRSHLAND thought not. Hirshland was Orrin Hatch's number two staffer on the Senate Judiciary Committee. He was barely 30, garrulous, and wicked smart, a former clerk for Supreme Court Justice Anthony Kennedy. He was also a diehard Republican, a free-marketeer, and therefore a man instinctively averse to government meddling in the affairs of commerce. But what Hirshland had learned about Microsoft's behavior troubled him deeply. Returning to Washington from Silicon Valley in the fall of 1997, he began calling up computer manufacturers such as Compaq and Internet service providers such as EarthLink to see if the allegations in the white papers about Microsoft's exclusionary practices held water. After a few weeks of poking around, Hirshland was convinced that "this was pretty damn serious." So he phoned the DOJ and arranged a meeting with Klein and his deputies.

On a gorgeous autumn day, Hirshland and the Judiciary Committee's chief counsel, Manus Cooney, walked down from Capitol Hill to the DOJ's Pennsylvania Avenue headquarters. Settling in at the long walnut table in the conference room that adjoined Klein's office, the Senate lawyers explained that they'd reached the conclusion that, at the very least, Microsoft warranted a serious investigation; and that, from what they could see, the DOJ wasn't conducting one. "They told us, 'If what you're basing this on are the Netscape white papers, forget about it,'" Hirshland recalled. "They said, 'A lot of those leads just didn't pan out. Reback? You can't trust that guy; he makes stuff up. And besides, we're not really sure that tying the browser to the operating system is illegal anyway.'"

Hirshland was prepared for the DOJ's resistance. Plucking a sheet of paper from his briefcase, he rattled off a list of the most blatantly questionable examples of Microsoft's conduct that he'd discovered. "What about all the exclusionary contracts?" Hirshland asked. "What about the OEMs? The ISPs? EarthLink? AOL? Gateway? Compaq?" Klein and his team fell silent. "The next thing you know," Hirshland remembered, "they pulled their notebooks out and were writing everything down."

After the meeting was over, Hirshland and Cooney walked back to the Hill. "Jesus Christ, Manus, that was all news to them!" Hirshland exclaimed. "Those guys aren't going to do jack."

This was not a unique assessment in the fall of 1997. Joel Klein had been around Washington a long time, and a fairly clear consensus had emerged as to what kind of an antitrust chief he was likely to be. The thumbnail sketch read like this: Klein was brilliant, scholarly, and sophisticated; also careful, cautious, and pathologically pragmatic. Politically astute and avowedly pro-business, he was nobody's idea of a tough-talking trustbuster in the tradition of Teddy Roosevelt or William Howard Taft. He would take only cases he knew he could win. And so, therefore, he'd steer clear of Microsoft.

In his early fifties, Klein was short and slight, with a perpetual tan and a shiny bald pate. He walked and talked softly, and seemed on first inspection to carry no stick at all. The son of a postman, he'd grown up in Queens, hoping to become a professional athlete. Robbed of that dream by the cruelties of genetics, Klein focused on academics, graduating magna cum laude from both Columbia University, where he majored in economics, and the Harvard Law School. After stints as a clerk to Supreme Court Justice Lewis Powell and as an advocate for the mentally ill, he went on to be a founding partner in a boutique Washington law firm specializing in complex trial and appellate work. In the 1980s, he earned a reputation as one of the most accomplished Supreme Court advocates of his generation, arguing 11 cases before the Court and winning eight.

Nearly three decades in the capital had turned Klein into a consummate Washington insider. He played tennis with Justice Antonin Scalia (Klein: "Nino can't quite believe that his authority as a Supreme Court justice doesn't mean he wins every shot") and was a certified FOB, having gotten to know President Clinton at Renaissance Weekends in the 1980s. Klein was also a close friend of the late David Ifshin, a well-known and much-beloved Washington lawyer who was an adviser to Clinton's 1992 Democratic primary campaign. When the very first story about the scandal that would come to be known as Whitewater appeared in *The New York Times* that year, Ifshin's instinct was to ask Klein to go to Little Rock and get to the bottom of the tangle of business dealings that would ultimately cause the Clintons so much heartache. But Ifshin's plan was scotched by the campaign, so Klein's skills remained untapped by the Clintons.

Not for long, however. When the deputy White House counsel, Vincent Foster, committed suicide in 1993, Klein was chosen by the President to be Foster's replacement. As Whitewater and its ancillary scandals mushroomed, Klein was a voice for sanity in the White House, arguing that the Clintons should make all the relevant documents public, and quickly. His probity kept him from being tainted by the scandals; and it earned him respect in some unlikely quarters, not least the offices of Orrin Hatch. But it also irritated many of Clinton's political operatives, as did his sometimes high-handed manner. When the time came, in 1996, to pick a new Solicitor General—a job Klein pined for—he was passed over. The antitrust post was his consolation prize.

Even that post was almost denied him. Having sailed through his confirmation hearings in the spring of 1997, he hit unexpectedly turbulent waters in the Senate when his name came up for final approval. The reason had little to do with Microsoft and much to do with telecommunications—in particular, with Klein's approval of the controversial $23 billion merger of the giant telephone companies Bell Atlantic and Nynex that April. Democrats were livid over the decision. "We've got an antitrust fellow here who rolls over and plays dead," said Democratic Senator Ernest Hollings of South Carolina, one of several who put a formal hold on his nomination. With *The New York Times* calling Klein "a weak nominee" and editorializing that the Clinton administration should withdraw him, and with his opponents obstinate and apparently committed, he seemed for a moment to be in serious trouble.

One of those opponents was Gary Reback. Already working to bypass Klein with his lobbying of the state AGs and Capitol Hill, Reback spent hours on the phone briefing the staff of Republican Senator Conrad Burns of Montana, chairman of the communications subcommittee of the Senate Commerce Committee and one of those with concerns about Klein's views on telecom policy—although unlike Democrats, Burns thought Klein was too tough, not too wimpy. Then Reback dispatched Susan Creighton to Washington to fan the Microsoft flames with the senator and his people. In a limited way, it worked: Burns was the first of the senators to put a hold on Klein's confirmation. But Klein had cultivated some crucial allies in the Senate, including Hatch, who regarded him as a man of high integrity even while disagreeing with him on many areas of policy. Once Klein had a chance to chat with Burns, and to whisper a few sweet somethings in the Montanan's ear, the senator relented, helping to clear the way for Klein's approval.

At Netscape, there were those, including chief counsel Roberta Katz, who feared that Reback's gambit might backfire (and who insisted that the company never officially opposed Klein's nomination). They were right to be worried. On Capitol Hill, where the only thing that moves faster than a senator sprinting toward a TV camera is confirmation scuttlebutt, word spread quickly about Reback's maneuvers, and found its way, inevitably, to the ears of Joel Klein. "Of course I heard," Klein said later. "It did make me smile when Microsoft said I was carrying Netscape's water. I had no loyalty or debt to them whatsoever—not that that kind of thing matters anyway. This isn't about politics. The principles are what matter."

Reback's finaglings may not have hurt Netscape's cause, but they certainly didn't help. Given their history, Klein had never been especially fond of Reback; now their relationship went from rocky to rotten. Some of Klein's colleagues recall that, for a time, he refused even to utter Reback's name, preferring instead to call him simply "that lawyer." The growing animosity between the two men—along with several episodes in which Reback seemed more intent on pursuing his own agenda than on advancing Netscape's—was a central factor in Katz's decision to hire Christine Varney, a former FTC commissioner and an old pal of Klein's, as Netscape's lead antitrust counsel in Washington, DC. "The situation wasn't good," Varney recalled. "Netscape found itself in a position where its principal antitrust lawyer had fought tooth and nail to defeat Joel's nomination, and now, lo and behold, Joel was the antitrust AG. As I said: not good."

Making matters worse for Netscape were the inclinations of many of the people surrounding Klein in the antitrust division. As was the case at every federal agency, the staff of the DOJ divided neatly in two: appointees and career bureaucrats, the latter outnumbering the former by a wide margin. Typically, career staffers, however talented and intelligent, tended to be skeptical and slightly jaundiced at best—and, at worst, unimaginably inert. After all, they had seen it all before. Not surprisingly, then, Klein's career staff seemed reluctant to go after Microsoft. Some thought the company had done nothing wrong. Some, having been badgered, hounded, and occasionally insulted by Reback for years, had no interest in lifting a finger to help one of his clients. Others seemed not to believe in antitrust enforcement at all. "Remember, we have people who came here during the Reagan administration," a DOJ official remarked.

Then there was Klein's second-in-command, Doug Melamed, an appointed official. Intellectual and rigorous, discreet and conscientious, Melamed made Klein look impetuous. If brevity is the soul of wit, Melamed was the soul of prudence. He had never met a nit he could not pick. His disposition on suing Microsoft: wait and see.

Amid the hypercautious consensus that held sway in the antitrust division there was, however, at least one dissenter: Dan Rubinfeld. Rubinfeld was a joint professor of law and economics at the University of California at Berkeley who had just taken over, at Klein's invitation, as the division's chief economist. Like his new boss, Rubinfeld was a small bald man—though the fringe of hair he retained was snow-white, while Klein's was dark brown—with a low-key demeanor and a high-pitched metabolism. He seemed at first glance no more likely than Klein to be eager to take a whack at Bill Gates. Quite the contrary. As a private-sector consultant, Rubinfeld had a lengthy record of appearing as an expert witness in corporate lawsuits, almost always on the side of the defense. In fact, years before, Rubinfeld had served as Microsoft's main expert in its prolonged, and successful, copyright litigation with Apple. "I had no anti-Microsoft bias when I came to Washington," he said. "I knew those people well. I respected them. I had spent a lot of time up there." Rubinfeld paused. "Though I don't expect I'll get another invitation to Redmond anytime soon."

When Rubinfeld arrived at the DOJ in the summer of 1997, he was somewhat surprised to find that the Microsoft investigation wasn't anywhere near the division's front burner. But on the assumption that it soon might be, he took a look at the Netscape white papers. "I wouldn't say they were very influential on the whole of the department," he said. "But I took them very seriously." Rubinfeld was impressed less by the catalog of abuses that the white papers accused Microsoft of perpetrating than by the clarity of Reback's and Creighton's strategic and economic analysis. Since the 1970s, antitrust economics had been dominated by the free-market orthodoxies brought into vogue by a group of University of Chicago scholars, including Milton Friedman and Ronald Coase, who argued that the market functioned so well—so effectively, so efficiently—that government intervention was unnecessary and even harmful. As an academic, Rubinfeld was one of a growing vanguard of "post–Chicago School" economists who rejected those orthodoxies; Garth Saloner, the Stanford professor who worked closely with Creighton and Reback, was another. Like Saloner, Rubinfeld had spent the past few years thinking hard about dynamic high-tech industries and had embraced the new economic ideas, from network effects to technological "lock-in," being advanced to explain how such industries work—ideas at the heart of the Netscape briefs.

To Rubinfeld, the white papers' central thesis seemed convincing: that the browser war was about more than browsers; it was about Microsoft protecting its operating-system monopoly. The more he studied the situation, the more he worried about the impending launch of the new version of Microsoft's browser, Internet Explorer 4 (IE4), which was designed to be more tightly bound to Windows than any previous browser had been. If the DOJ did nothing, Rubinfeld feared, the browser market might hit its "tipping point," with Netscape's share being driven rapidly toward irrelevance and Microsoft extending its monopoly into a vital new market.

Soon after he moved to the DOJ, Rubinfeld received a call from Reback, pleading to let him send Saloner in for a meeting. Rubinfeld readily agreed, in no small part because he wanted his warier colleagues in the division to hear what Saloner had to say. A few days later, Saloner showed up and took a seat on the small couch in Rubinfeld's cluttered office. Facing a clutch of DOJ economists and attorneys, Saloner, a native South African, held forth at length ("quite emotionally," Rubinfeld recalled) about what was really at stake in the battle between Microsoft and Netscape. "Nobody would fight over which browser is on the desktop," Saloner said. "This is about control of the gateway to electronic commerce. This is about somebody"—Microsoft—"potentially owning commerce. We're talking airlines, cars, banks, you name it."

For the next couple of hours, Saloner fielded a stream of questions, the most hostile and incredulous of which seemed to come from the lawyers. Saloner was surprised. All along, he and Reback and Creighton had assumed that the DOJ's economists, traditionally a fairly conservative bunch, were the biggest obstacle in their path. But now Melamed was grilling Saloner like a salmon filet, while Rubinfeld was quiet, and apparently quite receptive. What was Rubinfeld thinking? Saloner just couldn't tell.

After the meeting, Rubinfeld walked Saloner down the hall to the elevator. "He said, 'Thanks for coming, I really appreciate it. Really. I want you to know I'm concerned about this; it's my top priority.' I don't know why, but it seemed like he was trying to send me a message. When I got back to California, I said to Gary, 'Gee, I think we may be getting somewhere with Dan Rubinfeld.'"

They were. "What I wanted to tell him was, 'Garth, I'm on your side; you've confirmed everything I've been thinking already,'" Rubinfeld said later. "But it would have been totally inappropriate, so I kept my mouth shut."

WITH THE fall 1997 launch of IE4 just around the corner, the time was swiftly approaching to fish or cut bait. At the urging of Rubinfeld and a few other hawks within the division, Klein called Phil Malone in San Francisco and told him to send another CID to Microsoft. Broader than the document demands a year earlier, it focused particularly on the company's OEM licensing agreements with respect to the forthcoming browser. As reams of internal material from Microsoft began to pour in, the DOJ was startled not only by what the documents said but by the sheer baldness of how they said it. An email sent in late 1996 and another in early 1997, from Jim Allchin, Microsoft's top executive overseeing Windows, to Paul Maritz, stood out. In one, Allchin began, "I don't understand how IE is going to win. The current path is simply to copy everything that Netscape does packaging and product-wise. Let's suppose IE is as good as Navigator/Communicator. Who wins? The one with 80% market share . . . My conclusion is that we must leverage Windows more." In the other, he wrote, "you see browser share as job 1. The real issue deals with not losing control of the APIs on the client and not losing control of the end-user experience . . . We have to be competitive with [browser] features, but we need something more—Windows integration."

With the Allchin emails and a raft of other damning documents, the DOJ's long-dormant inquiry suddenly sprang to life. Soon the investigators also had in hand evidence supporting several key allegations leveled in the white papers and by Mike Hirshland about exclusionary contracts with OEMs and ISPs, and especially about Microsoft having threatened to revoke Compaq's Windows license if it removed IE in favor of Navigator.

Yet even then, a debate raged in the DOJ about what to do. There were many voices urging Klein to hold his fire; to investigate the matter further and bring a broad lawsuit, if that were justified, later. The most influential voice was that of Melamed, who argued that, however unsavory some of Microsoft's practices were, it was still unclear whether the company had actually done anything illegal. Melamed pointed out that the law regarding illegal "tying"— whereby a firm with a monopoly in one market forced consumers to buy another product as a condition of acquiring the first—was hazy and tended to favor defendants. And, despite the documents that had come in, he felt the evidence remained sketchy. If the DOJ planned to bring a major antitrust case against Microsoft, Melamed said, there was still a great deal of work to do.

Rubinfeld took a different tack. Under the 1995 consent decree between the DOJ and Microsoft, the company was explicitly prohibited from requiring OEMs to license any other product as a condition of their Windows licenses. But according to Microsoft's marketing plans, that was exactly what it intended to do with IE4. Indeed, the DOJ now had proof of something everyone in the computer industry had known for months: that this was Microsoft's practice with its current browser, IE3. Rubinfeld asked, Why not just sue the company for violating the consent decree and put off any decision about a broader case for the time being? "The browser market hasn't tipped yet, but it's really close," he said. By filing a narrow case immediately, perhaps the DOJ could keep that from happening.

In the end, of course, the decision was Klein's. For all his legal experience and expertise, he had entered the DOJ with scant background in antitrust. But in the past two years, Klein had absorbed enough to know not only that Melamed was absolutely right about the murkiness of the law on tying, but that the case would be made all the murkier by the subtle, abstract nature of the product in question: code. Still, it was hard for Klein to imagine a more compelling instance of illegal bundling than what Microsoft was planning with IE4, nor one more manifestly at odds with the letter and spirit of the consent decree. Moreover, he was aware that in the months since his Senate confirmation the political winds gusting around Microsoft had shifted appreciably. He knew that the contingent of state AGs looking into the company, which seemed to swell by the week, was charging ahead, and was likely to take action whether he did or not. After a few more conversations between his staff and Mike Hirshland and Manus Cooney, he knew the Senate Judiciary Committee was planning to hold hearings. He knew that Democrats on the Hill still had doubts about whether he had the stomach to joust with big business—and he was keen to dispel them. And, while he still was far from sure about bringing a broader suit, he sensed in his gut this was one he could win.

"I'll tell you what happened," said a government lawyer who was an admirer of Klein's. "For a year, the guys at the DOJ had dragged their feet and hadn't really investigated the thing. Then they finally dug into it a little and what they found was this flat-out case of tying, where Microsoft was saying, 'If you don't take IE, we're not going to give you Windows.' So here was Joel, saying to himself, 'I almost didn't get confirmed because people weren't sure I was tough enough. Well, here I've got this blatant violation—I'm going to court.' "

And so he did. On October 20, 1997, Klein stood next to Attorney General Janet Reno, with flashbulbs popping and cameras whirring, as she announced that the DOJ was not only seeking an injunction against Microsoft for violating the consent decree, but was asking a federal court to impose a fine of $1 million a day—the largest civil fine in Justice Department history—until the company stopped tying its browser to Windows. "Even as we go forward with this action today," Klein added, "we also want to make clear that we have an ongoing and wide-ranging investigation to determine whether Microsoft's actions are stifling innovation and consumer choice."

Out in Silicon Valley, Gary Reback heard that, laughed, and wondered if Klein was just blowing smoke. "This filing is a fine first step, but it's only a first step," Reback muttered over the phone. "All we can do is hope that it's just the first shoe to drop."

What no one could have guessed—not Reback, not Klein, and certainly not Bill Gates—was that, for Microsoft, it was the start of a hailstorm of footwear that would continue, amazingly and unabated, for the next three years.

Chapter 3

THE SHADOW OF THE MAN

THE MORNING the news from Washington broke, Gates was in the desert outside Phoenix, attending a high-end high-tech conference called Agenda at the famously opulent Phoenician hotel. Under normal circumstances, Gates moved easily among the Agenda crowd, for these were his people—the established leaders and the up-and-comers in an industry he had done as much as anyone to invent and then to place at the center of the world economy. Andy Grove, the chairman and CEO of Intel, was there; so were John Chambers of Cisco, Steve Case of AOL, Scott McNealy of Sun Microsystems, and the legendary venture capitalist John Doerr, all mingling in the hallways, speculating about what the DOJ's announcement might portend.

Yet the main subject of this feverish kibbitzing was nowhere to be found. For most of the day, Gates kept to his room, conferring with his lieutenants and lawyers by phone and dissecting the situation with Ann Winblad, the Silicon Valley venture capitalist who had once been his girlfriend. His only appearance in the grand ballroom where the conference program was taking place came late in the afternoon, when he stood for a while in the rear of the hall and heckled his rival Scott McNealy in a stage whisper, as Sun's CEO critiqued the government's action as too little too late.

That night, rather than mingle with the rest of computerdom's A-list, Gates retreated to a private supper with a handful of his friends: Dave Marquardt, the venture capitalist who had backed Microsoft and become a member of its board of directors; William Randolph Hearst III, scion to the storied newspaper family and now a Valley VC as well; the software entrepreneur Heidi Roizen; Winblad; and a few others. When the conversation turned to the DOJ, Gates explained in a tone at once dismissive and defiant why the government was wrong, why Microsoft was right, and why, in the end, he had nothing to worry about. He spoke at some length on these subjects, but it was a single sentence from Winblad that most perfectly encapsulated his attitude toward the lawsuit:

"These people have no idea who they're dealing with."

The next day, the man the government was dealing with took his turn on the Agenda stage. Dressed in a madras-plaid shirt and a pair of khakis, Gates laid out his company's arguments in unequivocal terms: that the consent decree specifically allowed Microsoft to develop "integrated products," and that IE was just such a product—fundamentally melded into Windows. "There's no magic line between an application and an operating system that some bureaucrat in Washington should draw. It's like saying that as of 1932, cars didn't have radios in them, so they should never have radios in them." The central question, Gates contended, was this: "Is one company excluded from innovation, or not?"

From the audience, Gates was asked about public opinion, about the growing sense, not only in Washington but in the industry at large, that Microsoft was wielding its power too wantonly. "You're sort of asking us if we're going to change, to start telling engineers, 'Slow down, slow down. Go home,' " Gates replied. "No, we're not."

Through most of the session, Gates was calm and collected, if occasionally curt. Then Rob Glaser, a former protégé of his at Microsoft and now the CEO of the Web media-streaming firm RealNetworks, stepped up to the microphone. "Bill, do you really think there is no limit to what should or should not be included in the operating system?" Glaser asked. "If there is a limit, who should set it? Microsoft? The Justice Department?"

"Look, look, this is called capitalism!" Gates snapped. "We create a product called Windows. Who decides what's in Windows? The customers who buy it."

For Gates, the Q & A at Agenda was a gentle preview of what lay ahead. With the onset of the consent-decree case, questions that previously had been raised only within the insular confines of the computer business and behind closed doors in Washington began to be asked in television newscasts and on the front pages of newspapers and magazines across the country. And although the DOJ was the primary provocateur, it wasn't the only one. The European Commission had opened an investigation of its own. In short order, the government of Japan would do the same. Ralph Nader, the old economy's hoariest rabble-rouser, was organizing an anti-Microsoft summit in Washington, featuring some of Redmond's most vocal foes. The most prominent of them was McNealy, who had just filed a separate lawsuit over Microsoft's use (or, as he contended, misuse) of the trendy Sun software technology Java, a suit in which Sun accused Microsoft of breach of contract, trademark infringement, false advertising, and unfair competition.

Thus in the fall of 1997 did Microsoft find itself subject to public scrutiny unlike any it had received in its 22-year history. The company's reaction was telling.

It began with Steve Ballmer, standing on a stage in San Jose a few days after the DOJ's filing, bellowing five ill-considered words that he would struggle to live down for years to come: "To heck with Janet Reno!" Then there was Microsoft's first formal response to the consent-decree case, a legal memorandum that labeled the DOJ's arguments "perverse," "uninformed," "misguided," "mislead-ing," "wrong," "just wrong," "simply wrong," and "without merit," and that suggested the government was not acting on behalf of consumers but at the behest of the firm's competitors. "The only persons in this country unaware that the DOJ is fully receptive to complaints about Microsoft," the document sneered, "is Rip Van Winkle."

Next came the business with the ham sandwich. When the DOJ issued its reply brief to Microsoft's memorandum, one passage fairly screamed out for attention amid the otherwise drowsy legal prose. "Microsoft asserts that 'integrated' means whatever Microsoft says it means," the brief said. "Indeed, in its discussions with the government before the Petition was filed, Microsoft flatly stated that its interpretation of the [consent decree] would enable it to require OEMs to put 'orange juice' or 'a ham sandwich' in the box with a PC preinstalled with Windows 95."

Microsoft had said exactly that. At a meeting with the DOJ just before Klein pulled the trigger, Richard Urowsky of the New York law firm Sullivan & Cromwell—Microsoft's primary outside legal counsel—let his flair for the dramatic run away with him.

Years later, Microsoft's legal team would still be fuming over what it called the government's "ham sandwich leak." "It was taken totally out of context," a Microsoft lawyer complained. "What Urowsky said was, 'We could put in a ham sandwich but nobody would buy it.' It was a perfectly legitimate thing to say. People wouldn't buy it if we put a ham sandwich in the OS. It was a metaphor for consumer choice." Unfortunately for Microsoft, Urowsky's rhetorical flourish, repeated endlessly in the press, was taken as another sort of metaphor entirely: a metaphor for the company's arrogance, for its unwillingness to acknowledge any limits to its power.

As autumn began to fade into winter, Microsoft was being roughed up in the national media, and its reaction grew only clumsier and more paranoid with each passing day. The trend reached new extremes at the company's annual shareholders meeting, when Gates lashed out at the "witch-hunt atmosphere" being ginned up by his enemies in the Valley and in DC. All through its history, Microsoft had been adroit, even masterful, at presenting a positive public image; now it looked as if it was melting down. The sight was so strange, so unexpected, I was sure the press accounts had to be exaggerated. There was simply no way Microsoft could really be that rattled.

Then I went to see Steve Ballmer.

Ballmer had long been Gates's best friend. They were classmates at Harvard—though Ballmer graduated while Gates dropped out—after which Ballmer worked briefly at Procter & Gamble and then spent a year at Stanford's business school before joining Microsoft in 1980. Ballmer wore a number of official hats at the company, but, unofficially, he had been Gates's number two through most of Microsoft's history. (Paul Allen, Gates's cofounder, left Microsoft in 1983, after learning he had Hodgkin's disease, from which he later recovered.) Even more unofficially, Ballmer played the role of Gates's mirror image: outgoing where Gates was shy, tactical where he was strategic, instinctual where he was contemplative. If Gates was Microsoft's ego, Ballmer— beefy, boisterous, a natural-born cheerleader—was its rampaging id. To say he was excitable was akin to saying Al Gore was wooden. Once, at a company pep rally, Ballmer shouted the chant "Win-Doze! Win-Doze!" at such decibels that he damaged his vocal cords.

Even so, I wasn't ready for what occurred when we met on a chill December afternoon in San Francisco, where Ballmer was delivering a speech to some customers. Sitting in a windowless conference room at the Westin St. Francis hotel, I asked Ballmer about an internal Microsoft document concerning its licensing of Java, which had come to light in the DOJ's investigation. In this document, Paul Maritz stated that the company's goal was to "get control of" and "neutralize" Java, which was then being sold as a kind of digital Esperanto that would let software coders create programs that could work without changes on any operating sys- tem—a raison d'être that was seen as posing a threat to Windows. Scott McNealy had told me he considered the document prima facie evidence that Microsoft had signed its Java contract in bad faith. I asked Ballmer if McNealy was right.

"Sun is just a very dumb company," Ballmer began.

"We always honored our license. We always intended to. We always have." His voice quickly rising, Ballmer continued, "Sun wasn't confused. We weren't coming in there saying, 'Hallelujah, brother! We love you, Sun!' We said, 'We don't like you as a com- pany'—nice people; I like Scott—'and you don't like us!' We said, 'Hey Sun, you want to get on the back of us and ride, baby, ride! You want on? OK, here's the terms!' "

Ballmer's face was beet-red now, and he was screaming so loudly that, had there been any windowshades, they would have been rattling. Up on his feet, leaning across the table so that his face was no more than six inches from mine, pounding his meaty fists on the tabletop so hard that my tape recorder leapt and skittered, he roared, "Nobody was ever one little teeny tiny bit confused that we and Sun had this wonderful dovetailing of strategic interests! Those sub-50-IQ people who work at Sun who believe that are either uninformed, crazy, or sleeping!"

I took this as a Yes.

"SUB-50 IQ people." "To heck with Janet Reno." "Ham sandwich." "Witch-hunt." Extending one long, thick middle finger to the United States government and to your competitors is not conventional behavior among the top executives of blue-chip companies. But then, Microsoft hadn't got where it was by behaving like most other blue-chips. Microsoft was different, self-consciously so. The differences had made it great—maybe the greatest corporation of the second half of the 20th century. But now, those very differences were driving it down a path toward the worst kind of trouble.

Microsoft was a very young company in almost every way that mattered. This was a fact easily obscured by the extent of its dominance, and by the head-snapping speed at which it had attained its power. As recently as 1990, Microsoft had been seen both within and without the computer industry as an exceptional outfit with enormous promise, but it was by no means the 800-pound ape it would soon become. Two things guaranteed its gorillahood. The first was Microsoft's success, with the introduction of Windows 3.0

in 1990 and Windows 3.1 in 1992, at knocking its graphical OS into decent shape, or at least decent enough shape for most consumers and corporations. The second was the roll-out in the early 1990s of Office, Microsoft's suite of productivity software (Word, Excel, PowerPoint), which commenced the process by which the company wiped out most of its rivals in the desktop applications market. As Roger McNamee, a Silicon Valley investor and former stock analyst who tracked the company for many years, put it, "That's when Microsoft went from being standard-setters, the best software company in the industry, to being gods in their own religion."

Microsoft was a young company in another important respect. From day one, Gates and his lieutenants had focused their recruiting on kids who were clever but green. For a long time, even after the company had swollen to tens of thousands of workers, the average age at Microsoft was under thirty. "We found it was easier to create a culture with people who were fresh out of school rather than hiring people from other companies and other cultures," Charles Simonyi, one of Microsoft's most senior and most revered programmers, once said. "You can rely on it, you can measure it, you can predict it, you can optimize it: you can make a machine out of it."

On the surface, there was nothing machinelike about life in Redmond, the details of which are, by now, familiar enough. The rambling campus, strewn with low-slung buildings and stands of evergreens. The free sodas. The shorts, backpacks, sandals, and flannel. By now, it's also well known that this supremely casual vibe belied a supremely aggressive culture, whose inhabitants liked to describe themselves as "hard-core." Populated by an army of young men (mainly), most of them unusually bright, many of them abnormally wealthy, working endless hours and pulling frequent all-nighters, Microsoft had always retained the air of a fraternity—a fraternity of rich eggheads, but a fraternity nonetheless. For years, Softies were wont to sport buttons that read FYIFV: Fuck You, I'm Fully Vested. Another favorite acronym, meant to suggest the lengths to which the company would go and the humiliations it would endure, in Ballmer's words, to "get the business, get the business, get the business," was BOGU: Bend Over, Grease Up.

Machismo, callowness, and profanity were not exactly unique to Microsoft; they were staples of life in Silicon Valley, too. What was unique, though, was the intense insularity of the Redmond culture. Situated hundreds if not thousands of miles from its competitors and partners, staffed mostly by folks who had never worked anywhere else, Microsoft was the frat house from another planet. Time and again, its engineers expressed apparently genuine surprise and a lack of comprehension that other high-tech companies harbored deep and abiding suspicions of Microsoft. Even Ballmer, a sharp guy despite all the hollering, was quoted in June 2000 in *Newsweek* saying, "People say a lot of things about us, but never has anyone said we're untrustworthy." Hello?

At the very heart of the Microsoft culture was technology—an assertion that will sound either axiomatic or ludicrous depending on your prejudices. To most Americans, Microsoft was more than a technology culture; it was *the* technology culture. In the Valley, however, the view was vastly different. There, even among some Microsoft allies, it stood as an article of faith that the company was incapable of innovating; that it was a copycat, a "fast follower," an assimilator of breakthroughs achieved elsewhere; that its products, despite their awesome popularity, were crashingly mediocre. But no matter what outsiders might have thought, no matter how much sniping and dismissiveness was hurled at them, Microsoft executives believed ardently that their company did in fact innovate. In support of that belief, they pointed to the extraordinary $3 billion the company spent each year on research and development, in areas ranging from voice recognition to artificial intelligence. At Microsoft, people did not take their pride in the company's marketing or salesmanship. They took it in the belief that they were great technologists, confecting great software.

Which was not to say that Microsoft didn't care about marketing and salesmanship. Since the early 1990s, the company had devoted vast resources to buffing its image, waging multimillion-dollar advertising campaigns, and carefully orchestrating press coverage to turn Microsoft, Windows, and Gates himself into household names. One of the clearest indications that Microsoft was becoming as much a marketing culture as an engineering culture came in 1994, when Gates hired Robert Herbold to be chief operating officer. A mild fellow of middling age, middling stature, and a certain bland charm, Herbold was a computer-science PhD who had risen to become the top marketing executive at Procter & Gamble. He spoke the lingo of branding, of corporate identity, of making "deposits" in the "key mental bank accounts" of customers. On arriving at Microsoft, Herbold quickly implemented the full complement of consumer-research techniques that he'd used at P&G, from extensive polling to focus groups.

As Microsoft began its recalcitrant flailing in the fall of 1997, I couldn't help wondering what Herbold was thinking. Here was his company, at which he was still a relative newcomer, violating every conceivable rule in the big-brand handbook of crisis management. Consider: What would McDonald's have done if it found itself in similar straits? What would Coca-Cola have done? Or Disney? Answer: Their CEOs would have appeared on the doorstep of the Justice Department and asked, in voices sugary with solicitude,

"What can we do to make the problem go away?" Yet this approach seemed never to have occurred to anyone of any consequence at Microsoft. A few months later, I visited Herbold in Redmond and asked if it made sense to interpret the company's belligerence as a sign that Microsoft had failed to internalize the notion that its success rested on its image as well as its technology.

"Yeah, it does," Herbold said. "But there comes a point in any company's life where, if a fundamental principle as to how you operate is being threatened, you have no choice but to stand tall." By temperament, Herbold was the antithesis of hard-core—he was soft-core. Yet, like Gates and seemingly everyone else up in Redmond, Herbold was adamant that the consent-decree case threatened to undermine the firm's ability to innovate. If thwarting that threat meant taking extreme and even potentially self-destructive measures, so be it.

"Always keep in mind, Microsoft is a company run by engineers," a departed Microsoft executive, himself an engineer, commented later. "Engineers like simplicity. They like clarity. They like rules. They don't like nuance. They don't like shades of gray. They're totally binary. Ones or zeros. Black or white. Right or wrong. Innovate or not innovate. That's how Bill sees the world. And if it's how Bill sees the world, it's how Microsoft sees the world.

"Remember, no one has ever accused Microsoft of being a democracy."

"THIS MORNING, just after 11:00, Michael locked himself in his office and he won't come out," begins Doug Coupland's 1995 novel *Microserfs,* still the most perceptive rendering of the Microsoft culture ever written. "Bill (Bill!) sent Michael this totally wicked flame-mail from hell on the e-mail system. Michael is certainly the most sensitive coder in Building Seven—not the type to take criticism easily. Exactly why Bill would choose Michael of all people to whale on is confusing.

"We figured it must have been a random quality check to keep the troops in line. Bill's so smart."

"Bill is wise."

"Bill is kind."

"Bill is benevolent."

"Bill, Be My Friend . . . *Please!*"

Nowhere in the annals of modern business did Emerson's aperçu that "an institution is the lengthened shadow of one man" hold more abundantly true than at Microsoft. From the moment the company was founded, everything about it—good and bad, strong and weak—had been a pure crystalline reflection of Gates's mind, his personality, his character. In the computer industry, few founders had been able or willing to stick with their firms as the companies grew, guiding them from birth to maturity. Scott McNealy was a notable exception; so was Larry Ellison, of Oracle. But although both McNealy and Ellison were forceful and dynamic CEOs, neither had come close to exerting the type of hold over his company that Gates maintained over Microsoft.

The feelings that many Microsoft employees had for their boss went beyond respect or loyalty or admiration and crept right up to the brink of infatuation: in one way or another, everyone in Redmond seemed to have a crush on Bill. Gates inspired this intense following without being, in any conventional sense, a charismatic or especially winning figure. What he was, was very smart, and in the Microsoft culture that he himself had engendered, smartness was valued above all. To be deemed smart—or, better still, supersmart—was to be awarded the greatest accolade in the Microsoft lexicon. And to be paid the compliment by Gates himself . . . that was the true and only heaven. "There are probably more smart people per square foot right here than anywhere else in the world," the former top Microsoft executive Mike Maples said. "But Bill is just smarter."

The slavish fealty accorded Gates at Microsoft drew gales of derision from critics and competitors. Netscape's counsel, Roberta Katz, contended that it was the "blind obedience, the willingness to suspend all judgment and follow the party line, all this zombielike devotion to the Maximum Leader" that led Microsoft inexorably to its fate in court. "It's the whole voice-of-God thing," said Bill Joy, Sun's chief scientist and a longtime nemesis of Gates. "At Microsoft, they're always asking, 'What would Bill think?' As if Bill is the oracle. As if Bill always knows best. It's very hard to be creative in that kind of environment, and it's even harder to do clean-sheet work, because all the old stuff is the oracle's stuff, and who's going to tear that up and start fresh? It's why they can't innovate no matter how many smart people they hire." Gates, said Joy, was "the low priest of a low cult."

Gates had always been prone to caricature, which made his leadership of Microsoft all the harder to parse. In the 1980s and much of the 1990s, his PR handlers succeeded magnificently in having him portrayed in a flattering but one-dimensional fashion: he was the original golden geek, a brilliant, bespectacled non-threatening nebbish, whose firm was creating neat software to bring the wonders of computing to the masses. After becoming the richest man on the planet, in the mid-1990s, Gates underwent by necessity a slight image upgrade, in which he was recast as a still-brilliant, still-benevolent captain of industry and technological visionary. Now, with his company being dragged into court and with controversy swirling all around, he was being turned by his foes into another caricature: the postmodern robber baron, whose sensibilities were attuned to the new economy but whose greed and rapacity were reminiscent of the old.

None of these portraits did even rough justice to the multi-sided figure poised at Microsoft's helm. Indeed, if Bill Clinton was the priapic president, Bill Gates was the prismatic CEO: a man who reflected a wide array of sometimes contradictory qualities—brusque but reticent, imperious but insecure, far-seeing but myopic—depending on what day of the week it was and which angle he happened to be sighted from.

Gates himself cringed at another of the cartoon versions of his persona—"the ultracompetitor," he called it. But in this case, the cartoon captured something essential. Competition compelled Gates; it propelled him forward. It had been that way since he was growing up in upper-crust suburban Seattle in the 1960s. As a kid, Gates was reedy and obsessive, fixating on his passions—books and computers—at the expense of everything else, including bathing, grooming, and other aspects of personal comportment. Born in 1955, he had two sisters, and together with his parents they formed a family that was unnervingly energetic. The Gateses seemed determined to fill every spare moment with an organized activity, and to turn every organized activity into some form of contest. Sports, games, puzzles, quizzes, races—you name it, they did it, and ceaselessly. "I really like Bill's family," a former Microsoft executive once remarked. "But it would be nice if you could talk to them once in a while when they weren't in a human pyramid."

Gates was close to his mother, Mary, a regent at the University of Washington and a chairwoman of the United Way, who died of breast cancer in 1994. But he had been, and he remained, very much his father's son. William Gates Jr. (Microsoft's chairman was William Henry Gates III, which accounted for his childhood nickname, Trey) was one of Seattle's most prominent lawyers and civic brahmins. He was tough-minded, gracious, and free of ostentation. Powerfully built, standing six-foot-six, and powerfully connected, he fostered in his son an enduring fascination with the law. For a time it seemed possible that young Bill might become a lawyer, which was what his father had vaguely hoped for. Steve Ballmer recalled that some of his first serious conversations with Gates when they met at Harvard were about the law; in particular, Ballmer remembered his friend talking animatedly about an antitrust case involving Wonder Bread in which Gates's father had played a role.

The elder Gates was also an active player in the political arena in Washington State. Senators, congressmen, and governors came to dinner at the family's house when Bill was a boy. In the summer of 1972, the father helped his son land a job as a congressional page on Capitol Hill. Gates had a ball, collecting the signatures of all 100 senators and making a few bucks, he recalled, by "cornering the market" on Tom Eagleton campaign buttons and reselling them after Eagleton withdrew from the vice-presidential slot on that year's Democratic ticket. Between politics, the law, and business, Gates inherited from his father a far more conservative and establishmentarian outlook than most observers have ascribed to him. In this light, it would come as no surprise that two of his close friends outside Microsoft—and he had very few—would be Warren Buffett and Katherine Graham, both venerable symbols of the old elite.

There was nothing establishmentarian, however, about Gates's decision, in the summer of 1975, to quit Harvard after just two years and team up with his high-school chum Paul Allen to start what was known at first as Micro-Soft. But Gates was in love with computers and with the idea of personal computing—a wild, borderline lunatic concept at the time. Together, he and Allen wrote the software for one of the first primitive home computers, the MITS Altair. At 19, Gates was skinny, smelly, unkempt, unsocialized. An archetypal hacker, that is, except for one thing. The hackers of the 1970s were grounded in academia, communitarian in their philosophy, and saw software as something to do for fun. Gates was entrepreneurial, an instinctive capitalist, and saw software as a way of making money.

Gates's hacker roots became a central element of his public legend, which depicted him as a technological genius. The legend elicited eye-rolling (and less charitable responses) in computing circles, where his technical gifts were regarded almost universally as solid but unexceptional. "Neither Bill nor Paul was tremendously technically sophisticated when they started Microsoft, and they're not now," said David Liddle, the former director of Allen's now-defunct think tank, Interval Research, and a friend of both men. In 25 years working in software, Gates personally had made no significant contributions to computer science. He held but one patent. Yet at Microsoft, top-flight scientists spoke of his technical fluency in tones of awe. Gates, they suggested, was a fox and not a hedgehog; a technologist whose strength was breadth, not depth. Craig Mundie, a senior Microsoft executive who in 2000 spent more time than anyone discussing the future of technology with Gates, explained, "Bill's great gift is synthesis: his ability to accumulate a huge amount of information and then synthesize it on a grand scale."

In a way, the myth of Gates as a mighty technologist overshadowed his rightful claim to genius as a businessman. Of course, Gates was often credited, and justly so, with being among the first to discern that software could be the basis of an enterprise; with having appreciated that software, not hardware, was where the big money would be made in personal computing; and with having shrewdly persuaded IBM, when it asked Microsoft to provide an operating system for its first PC, in 1980, to allow his firm to retain the rights to that software, MS-DOS. But Gates's insights were far more sweeping than that. Before he arrived on the scene, the computer industry had always been organized vertically. That is, it consisted of companies like IBM and DEC that built their own machines, designed and manufactured their own microchips, and developed their own operating systems and applications, all of them proprietary. Side by side with Intel's Andy Grove, Gates envisioned a different structure, a horizontal structure, in which specialized competition would take place in each layer of the industry: chip company versus chip company, software company versus software company, computer company versus computer company. He figured out, again with Grove, that the position of maximum power and profit in this new structure came from owning one of two critical industry standards: the OS or the microprocessor. And, finally, he understood that Microsoft's control of the OS standard could be leveraged in ways that would give the company enormous advantages in competing for other software markets.

Gates's strategic foresight was twinned to a tactical discipline and a single-mindedness that were unusually fierce. For a long time, he seemed oblivious to the marginalia of corporate life, the perks and status symbols, that distract so many major-league executives. His office was modest, exactly twice as large as those of junior employees. He disdained titles. He flew coach. And while he never suffered from a deficit of ego, he was relatively immune to intellectual vanity, keeping close tabs on ideas and trends gaining currency beyond Microsoft's borders. "He carefully reads the wind and weather," Liddle said, "and he does not have false pride about admitting he's wrong"—as he did, famously and remarkably, in turning Microsoft around in the mid-1990s after initially underestimating the significance of the emergence of the Internet.

Nor was he prone to technical vanity. Where other high-tech CEOs often squandered time and money in pursuit of perfect, elegant solutions, Gates refused to let the great be the enemy of the good, or even to let the good be the enemy of the minimally serviceable. Over and over, he attacked new markets with the same pragmatic sequence of moves: dive in fast with a half-assed product to establish an early foothold, improve it steadily (even Microsofties joked that the company never got anything right until version 3.0), then use clout, low prices, and any other means necessary to gobble up a dominant share of the market. About the extent of Microsoft's appetites, Gates and his lieutenants were unabashed. "My job is to get a fair share of the software applications market," Mike Maples said back in 1991. "And, to me, that's 100 percent."

Gates's hunger for new conquests left a trail of bloody bodies strewn in Microsoft's wake. Digital Research. WordPerfect. Novell. Lotus. Borland. Apple. "Bill [had an] incredible desire to win, and to beat other people," the former Microsoft executive Jean Richardson recalled in the popular PBS documentary *Triumph of the Nerds*. "At Microsoft, the whole idea was that we would put people under."

But while Gates's style of competition was at once relentless and remorseless, it seemed to be fueled as much by anxiety as by cruelty. Long before Andy Grove made "Only the paranoid survive" the watchphrase of Silicon Valley, Gates was living the mantra at Microsoft. "Bill runs scared much more than people think," said Will Hearst, one of Gates's closer friends. "He does what he does out of fear, not sadism. The history of business is full of guys looking out the 50th-story window of their corporate headquarters, seeing some little pipsqueaks down below, and going, 'Oh, forget it; how could they ever threaten us?' And then getting their clocks cleaned. Bill just knows he doesn't want to be one of those guys."

Or, as Gates himself said to me one day in his office, "The fact that you can't name the place you're going to die doesn't mean you shouldn't pay attention to your health."

THE MORTALITY of skyscraper-dwelling overlords was a phenomenon with which Gates was intimately familiar. When his company's partnership with IBM began, Big Blue was arguably the exemplary corporation of the modern age. It was 3,000 times the size of Microsoft and had defined commercial computing for three decades. "It's easy to forget how pervasive IBM's influence over this industry was," Gates recalled. "When you talk to people who've come into the industry recently, there's no way you can get it into their heads: IBM was the environment." Then the men from Armonk met Gates, and everything changed. By the early 1990s, not only had IBM's hegemony been shattered, but the company was on the ropes—losing billions of dollars a year, laying off employees by the thousands, struggling for its very survival. Meanwhile, Microsoft was ascendant. In January 1993, it surpassed IBM in market value and never looked back; a few weeks later, IBM's board tried in vain to recruit Gates to become the company's chairman. The role reversal was complete: Microsoft was the environment.

The fall of IBM was a seminal experience for Gates and Ballmer, shaping their perspectives in countless ways, both obvious and subtle. "If you asked me where I learned more about business than anyplace else, I wouldn't point to school, I wouldn't point to my two years at Procter & Gamble, I wouldn't point to Microsoft," Ballmer said. "I would point to my ten years working with IBM." With the passage of time, he and Gates came to extol and even to emulate IBM's strengths—its devotion to research, its attentiveness to customers. But during Microsoft's formative period, their opinions were somewhat less favorable.

"We hated IBM," said Peter Neupert, an ex-Microsoft executive who worked closely with Big Blue on the joint development of the operating system OS/2 and then became the CEO of the start-up drugstore.com. "We hated their decision-making process, which was incredibly bureaucratic and stilted. We hated their silly rules and requirements: the red tape was unbelievable. And we had zero respect for their engineering talent. The core of Microsoft is: Great talent matters. We had a great team; theirs was big, slow, and sloppy." (Among Microsoft's OS/2 coders, IBM stood for Incredible Bunch of Morons.) "Bill always believed small teams were better, and that belief was magnified by seeing how IBM worked. As a result, we fought bigness at every stage. We had no processes. We had no planning department. Anything that would slow decisions down was rejected by design. Bill wanted to preserve a freewheeling style, where you made decisions fast and didn't get bogged down. It all comes from his programmer orientation. The people who were rewarded most at Microsoft were cowboys and misfits— the guys IBM would never hire. That was a point of pride."

If IBM provided Gates with an object lesson in the perils of gigantism, it also offered him a case study in how debilitating a constant fear of government intrusion could be. From the early 1950s until the early 1980s, IBM had been continually under investigation by, or in litigation with, federal antitrust authorities. In 1956, the company had signed a consent decree that forced it to license its patents at a "reasonable" price to all comers; and in 1969, the DOJ had launched its landmark 13-year lawsuit accusing IBM of illegal monopolization of the computer industry—a lawsuit which, despite being dropped in 1982, saddled the company with a legacy of competitive restraint and legalistic caution that played no small part in its vulnerability to the PC revolution that Microsoft spearheaded. "Every decision they made—on products, packaging, marketing— was based at least in part on legal constraints or perceived legal constraints," Neupert recalled. "It was screwy." And it made a large and lasting impression on the boys from Redmond. "Bill thought a lot about it," Neupert said. "In dealing with IBM, they'd have lawyers in technical meetings. Ludicrous! So the question for us was: How important are we going to let the lawyers be at Microsoft?"

Gates's answer was: not very. It would prove fateful. In 1985, the year before Microsoft went public, its legal department consisted of Bill Neukom and two other employees. Over the next 15 years, the legal department would steadily expand to more than 400 employees, 150 of them attorneys. Yet despite all those warm bodies, through the 1980s and most of the 1990s Microsoft failed to adopt an official antitrust-compliance policy or a comprehensive antitrust-training regime for its employees. After the DOJ filed its case, Microsoft's lawyers were at pains to deny this. They produced documents listing an array of programs (Executive Competition Counseling, Consent Decree Training, Legal Road Shows) intended "to ensure that Microsoft employees understand and comply with legal obligations under US and other antitrust laws." Antitrust training had even been incorporated into the "Microsoft 101 training vehicle" for all new employees—although that incorporation took place in 1999, well after the company's imbroglio with the government began.

Ballmer insisted that Microsoft had had "antitrust audits, antitrust reviews, antitrust training" since the mid-1980s. "Now, do we train every Tom, Dick, and Harry in the company?" he asked. "No. But it's not every Tom, Dick, and Harry that's making the decisions." Yet in dozens of interviews with current and former Microsoft executives, I found few who could recall having received antitrust training, and of those who said they could, even fewer who remembered anything they'd been taught, beyond the vague instruction to "obey the law." In the fall of 1998, *Business Week* reported that Mike Maples had only recently been enlisted to draft a code of conduct for the company—an assignment he acknowledged having failed to complete. "I can't find the principles that would mean the world would like us more," Maples said. "We can't tell people not to be so aggressive or don't compete so hard." And a few months later, on the stand in the trial, Paul Maritz would testify under oath that he knew of no formal antitrust-compliance policy at Microsoft.

To trustbusters such as Joel Klein, Gates's unwillingness to implement a thorough antitrust program was a plain sign of his immaturity as a CEO. "Major corporations in America have these things—they just do," Klein said. "It's just sensible; it's just prudent." Even in the high-tech industry, the absence of such a program at Microsoft raised eyebrows, including those of Gates's ally, Andy Grove. Grove, who would no more have conceded that Intel had a monopoly on PC microprocessors than he would have admitted a sneaking fondness for New Age management techniques, had instituted a far-reaching antitrust regimen at his company as far back as 1986. For years thereafter, he periodically raised the issue with Gates and complained to other Intel executives about Gates's "pigheaded" refusal to follow suit. Yet something more complex and calculating than mere pigheadedness was at work. To Gates's way of thinking, being without an antitrust program may have carried with it certain legal risks, but the risks of enacting one were even greater. "Bill's thought was that once we accept even self-imposed regulation, the culture of the company will change in bad ways," a former senior Microsoft executive explained. "It would crush our competitive spirit."

Gates put an even finer point on his fear. Talking privately once with another of the industry's top CEOs, who had asked him if Microsoft was taking sufficient precautions to ward off government scrutiny, Gates said flatly, "The minute we start worrying too much about antitrust, we become IBM."

Years later, when bemused analysts and commentators tried to explain the behavior that got Microsoft into such hot water with the government, one theory in particular came into fashion: after years of seeing itself as David, the feisty underdog doing battle with the industry's behemoths, Microsoft had failed to realize that somewhere along the way it had become Goliath—and that Goliaths were subject to a stricter set of rules than Davids were. The truth, however, was slightly different. Gates hadn't failed to recognize anything. Having witnessed the collapse of IBM up close and personal, he was determined not to allow Microsoft to fall prey to a similar syndrome, and had repeatedly taken explicit steps to preserve the company's Davidian attitudes and attributes in spite of its mass and muscle. The result was a culture built on a willing suspension of disbelief; a culture whose official stance was neatly—and ridiculously—summed up in 1997 by COO Bob Herbold thus: "Think about the technology business in its broadest sense. Microsoft is a small but important player in that very large industry."

That was the company's public posture. In private, though, when the man who ran Microsoft let down his guard, he betrayed no confusion about what he and his company had become. A close friend of Gates's recalled a dinner with him and his then-fiancée (and later his wife) Melinda French back in 1993. "We were talking about Clinton, who'd just been elected, and Bill was saying blah, blah, blah about whatever the issue was," this friend remembered. "Then Bill stopped and said, 'Of course, I have as much power as the president has.' And Melinda's eyes got wide, and she kicked him under the table, so then he tried to play it off as a joke. But it was too late; the truth was there. If Bill ever thought of himself as a scrappy little guy, he didn't anymore."

BY THE middle of the 1990s, Gates may have been as powerful as the president in some ways, yet he remained as paranoid as a speed freak at the end of a long and extravagant binge. The proximate cause of his paranoia was Netscape. In May 1995, in a memo entitled "The Internet Tidal Wave," Gates argued that the start-up's browser held the potential to "commoditize the underlying operating system"—Windows. What worried him, Gates explained later, wasn't merely the threat posed by the browser or other forms of "middleware" (software that fell short of being a full OS but which might still be a platform for applications) but the sudden momentum Netscape had gained in the industry. "Lightning struck," Gates said. "There was a belief that they were the exciting thing, they were the coming company. You'd go to their developer conferences, go to Marc Andreessen's press conferences, read the article about what flavor of pizza he ordered. That phenomenon was getting developers to pay a lot of attention to the Netscape browser." He added, "Expectations are a form of first-class truth: If people believe it, it's true." And people were believing in Netscape.

As was Microsoft, in a sense. When Andreessen and his colleagues first started talking about turning their lean little browser into a full-blown platform, the idea struck Gates and Ballmer as perfectly plausible—not surprisingly, since Microsoft itself had pulled off the same trick. "Let me tell you a story," Ballmer told a reporter at the time. "Once upon a time there was a piece of software that was an extension of an operating system, and it had a nice little user interface, and it had some programming interfaces, and people kind of liked it. One day, the thing that it was built on top of wasn't all that important anymore, and it kind of got subsumed inside of the thing that was originally an extension." This tale, Ballmer continued, was the story of what had happened in the course of 10 years with Windows, which was originally nothing more than an application running on top of DOS. "If I wanted to compete with Microsoft," Ballmer concluded, "I would do what Netscape is doing. I'd say, I'll build on top of Windows and I'll take their future away from them."

The only thing that surprised Microsoft about Netscape's strategy was the brazenness with which the upstarts shouted it to the world. Nathan Myhrvold said, "There's a good analogy to bicycle racing. In bicycle racing, you don't want to be first until the end. What you want to do is draft the guy in front of you. And then, in the last minute, you dart out. The middleware gambit is about drafting the leader." Yet here was Andreessen baldly and publicly proclaiming in the summer of 1995 that Netscape's plan was to reduce Windows to "a poorly debugged set of device drivers." "They didn't save it up," Myhrvold said. "They fucking pulled up alongside us and said, 'Hey, sorry, that guy's already history.' "

Netscape's brashness drove Redmond into a rage. The day after Andreessen's quote appeared in the press, John Doerr, the venture capitalist who bankrolled Netscape and sat on its board, received a bone-chilling email from the Microsoft executive Jon Lazarus, a friend of Doerr's and one of Gates's key advisers. In its entirety, the email read: "Boy waves large red flag in front of herd of charging bulls and is then surprised to wake up gored."

Over the next three years, Microsoft would impale Netscape on an assortment of horns. But its very first thrust was the one that led to the consent-decree case: the decision to bundle and then integrate IE into Windows. Even apart from its effect on Netscape, Gates firmly believed that Web browsing was a natural addition to any OS, one that would serve consumers and make computing easier. Adding IE to Windows for free, he said, was "the most defensible thing we've ever done." It was also indisputably legal, he maintained. When Microsoft had bargained with the DOJ (and the European Commission, which was simultaneously pursuing its own investigation) over the consent decree in 1994, Gates had taken great care to ensure that the provision on tying was worded broadly enough to give Microsoft unfettered freedom to put new features into Windows. At one point, when Neukom presented Gates with a proposed draft of the decree which stated that Microsoft would not be prohibited from "developing integrated products which offer technological advantages," Gates barked, "Remove those last four words!"

Gates, Neukom, and Microsoft's legal team were therefore stunned when the DOJ filed the 1997 consent-decree case. It seemed to them that the Feds were either woefully unaware of the negotiating history of the decree (a deal that was cut under Anne Bingaman, Klein's predecessor) or had willfully chosen to ignore it. Equally maddening was the premise of the DOJ's claim: that because Explorer was distributed to PC makers on a different disk from Windows, and because it was also marketed as a stand-alone product, it was by definition not "integrated." At a meeting between the DOJ and Microsoft's lawyers that fall, Klein held aloft the two disks and said, "See? Two separate products." To Microsoft, the gesture was glaring evidence of Klein's technological cluelessness. Once IE and Windows were installed together, they fused into one seamless whole; the fact that they were distributed on separate disks, as software products frequently are, was irrelevant. "It's all just bits," Neukom said. "Antitrust law isn't about how you distribute the bits; it's about how the bits relate to each other."

Klein may have been clueless about the commingling of code, but the DOJ's argument found a friendly pair of ears on the large round head of Thomas Penfield Jackson. Jackson was the gruff, grandfatherly federal judge who had somehow lucked into hearing the consent-decree case. After nearly two months of legal volleys, on December 11 he issued a stopgap split decision that cut sharply against Microsoft. On one hand, Jackson said, the company had offered a "plausible interpretation" of the term "integrated" and a "reasonable explanation" as to why its behavior was kosher under the consent decree; so the judge rejected the government's motion to fine Microsoft $1 million a day. On the other hand, although Jackson remained undecided on the merits of the case and needed more time to sort out the issues, he found that the DOJ "appears to have a substantial likelihood of success" and that "the probability that Microsoft might also acquire yet another monopoly in the Internet browser market is simply too great to tolerate indefinitely until the issue is finally resolved." And so Jackson handed down a preliminary injunction ordering Microsoft to "cease and desist" from requiring PC makers to install IE as a condition of their Windows licenses. Until the case was decided, Microsoft was to offer them a browser-free version of the OS.

Microsoft felt that Jackson's order put the company in an impossible bind. In its filings in the case, Microsoft had said again and again that taking the browser code out of Windows would break the OS—it would no longer boot properly. Yet removing that code was precisely what Jackson was telling them to do. In a conference room down the hall from Gates's office in Building 8 on Microsoft's campus, the CEO and his minions mulled over the dilemma. Naturally, the company would appeal Jackson's decision immediately. But what to do in the meantime? After a grueling series of weekend meetings, the Microsoft executives reached a conclusion that was flagrant, provocative, and ill-considered. To comply with the judge's order, they would offer OEMs a choice of either a two-year-old version of Windows without IE or a current version that simply didn't function. That is, no choice at all. At the session on Sunday afternoon when Gates approved the decision, everyone concurred that Microsoft was adhering precisely and carefully to the letter of the law. Even so, one Redmond bigshot acknowledged the inevitable: "We're going to get hammered."

Did they ever. In a blistering motion filed in response by the DOJ, the government accused the company of a "naked attempt to defeat the purpose of the Court's Order" and a "flagrant disgregard" for Jackson's authority. It asked again that the judge find Microsoft in contempt. Several weeks later, Klein was still spitting mad over what he saw as a shocking disrespect for the rule of law. "The federal court comes down with this decision and they somehow think, without coming to us, without going to the court, that the answer is to put out a product that breaks?" Klein sputtered. "Usually the phrase 'contempt of court' is metaphoric. In this case, it was literal."

Two days after the DOJ's motion, Jackson summoned the parties to his courtroom in Washington, DC. Before a packed gallery, the sixtysomething judge leaned into the microphone and made an unlikely statement: he and his clerks had been doing some hacking. The day before, Jackson said, he had instructed a technician to run the "uninstall" process on Windows 95 to try to make IE disappear. After "less than 90 seconds," he continued, a message flashed on screen that Explorer was no longer operative—yet Windows was functioning "as flawlessly as before." Jackson growled, "If the process is not that simple, I'd like to have it refuted by any evidence Microsoft wishes to introduce." A dramatic pause. "I want to know whether to believe my eyes."

A few weeks later, in mid-January, after another hearing in which Jackson heaped scorn on Microsoft and its witnesses, the company backed down. In consultation with the DOJ, it agreed to offer computer makers a version of Windows that still contained some IE code, but in which the browser was disabled and hidden from view. Through all the trouble that followed, Gates and his lawyers would refuse to admit that this was what they should have done in the first place, not least because most PC manufacturers would have continued (and in fact did continue) to take the version of Windows that included IE. "Do I wish we'd found a more politically, personally, atmospherically palatable response?" one of Microsoft's senior attorneys mused. "Sure. But we couldn't then and we still can't."

"Maybe we should have gone to the DOJ and said, Hey, this won't work. Why don't we go to the judge and try to figure it out?" another Microsoft lawyer allowed. "But we were in an adversarial situation, remember. And we were trying to make a point that was lost on the court."

THE PRICE of making that point would prove to be greater than Microsoft could ever have imagined. Two and a half years later, when Judge Jackson issued his order that the company be split up, he cited its "illusory" and "disingenuous" compliance with his injunction in the consent-decree case as probative evidence that Microsoft was "untrustworthy" and that conduct remedies alone weren't sufficient to rein in its power. And even in the short term, the damage was severe. In America and abroad, in the news columns and in editorial cartoons, criticism, sarcasm, and even mockery of Microsoft suddenly appeared where once there had been little besides adulation. For the first time ever, Ballmer acknowledged, the company's polling and focus groups had begun to show that the negative publicity was taking a toll on Microsoft's image. "It's not cataclysmic, but it's clear," he told *The Wall Street Journal.*

At the same time, Microsoft's insolence seemed only to have emboldened the DOJ and the states as they turned their attention to the question of whether to launch a full-scale antitrust action against the company. If anyone had a doubt that they were serious, one piece of news should have instantly obliterated it: the news that Klein had retained David Boies, the famed New York litigator who had successfully defended IBM against the government's antitrust charges in the 1970s and 1980s, as a consultant to the DOJ.

The gathering storm was unlike anything Gates had ever weathered. For all his social unease and childlike (some would say childish) tendencies, he was anything but naive. He was not unused to the rough-and-tumble. He reveled in competition, hard-edged competition, complete with low blows and high-flying elbows. Contrary to the popular perception of high technology as an industry rife with fresh-faced idealists and barefoot billionaires—an image with astonishing resilience, even after the wretched excesses and over-the-top moneygrubbing of the dot-com boom—the computer business had never been a pretty place. It had always had more than its share of personal vilification, ego-driven vendettas, and postindustrial espionage. Competitors had been assailing Gates and his company in every fashion imaginable for more than a decade. And although he could be thin-skinned, and although he had a tendency to blow his stack, and although he would lash out at the anti-Microsoft posse when its members took potshots at him in the media or behind his back, Gates was well aware that all this was part of the program. And, of course, he gave as good as he got.

But what was happening now ... this was different. This wasn't business. This was the US government, an adversary not unknown to him, but one against whose slings and arrows his defenses weren't nearly so robust. In the months ahead, it would be repeated ad nauseam that, for a firm of its importance and stature, Microsoft had paid dangerously little attention to politics over the years. This was true: as recently as 1995, the company had no government-affairs office in Washington, DC. Yet Gates didn't think of himself as a political innocent. He had never been partisan, but who was anymore? He had issues he cared about—trade, immigration, encryption, taxes—and had lobbied on behalf of. He had even dabbled a bit in the art of the schmooze. He had golfed with Bill Clinton on more than one occasion. He had dined with Newt Gingrich back when that meant something. He had hosted Al Gore on a visit to Microsoft. (For a time, Gore's daughter Karenna had worked at the Microsoft-funded online magazine *Slate*.) More to the point, Gates believed that he and Microsoft had delivered to the Clinton administration perhaps the greatest political gift of the postwar era: the new economy. Who had done more than he had to spark the PC revolution? What company had done more to provide the underpinnings of the information age? Directly and indirectly, Microsoft had generated untold wealth. In Windows, it had built a platform on which much of the high-tech economy stood. It had created products on which millions of workers relied. It had spurred the Nasdaq to improbable heights. And now, after all this, after all he had done, the government that should have been showering him with praise and gratitude was casting him as a villain, a scoundrel, a grasping monopolist. It was crazy, infuriating. And it was starting to get under his skin.

As the consent-decree contretemps wound to a close, the blind outrage that had colored Gates's mood for months remained intact, but increasingly it was overshadowed by something darker. Among his small circle of close friends, word began to spread that Gates had fallen into a deep blue funk. "His own government suing him, that's not chocolate sundae," his father would later tell *Newsweek*. "He was concerned, he was angry, he was distracted from things he'd rather be doing." Actually, it was much worse than that. According to one old friend, "He was going through a period where he kept saying, 'I hate my job. I hate my life. I hate this situation. I don't know what to do.' "

Seeing Gates demoralized to the point of despondency disturbed his friends. It also worried the Microsoft board. On January 24, the directors (Paul Allen, ex–Microsoft president Jon Shirley, venture capitalist Dave Marquardt, Mattel CEO Jill Barad, financier William Reed, and Hewlett-Packard executive Richard Hackborn) gathered for their monthly meeting. It was a gray Saturday just 72 hours after the company had come to terms with Jackson and the DOJ on the preliminary injunction, and the board expected that much of the meeting would be taken up with discussion of the consent-decree case and the broader suit that the government was known to be contemplating. At least a few of Microsoft's directors were hoping to raise another issue as well: the possibility of promoting Ballmer to president from his current position as executive vice president of sales and support—in order, one board member later confided, "to take some of the burden off Bill's shoulders." Yet it was only when Gates began to speak that anyone fully realized how great the burden had become.

Looking haggard, as though he hadn't slept in days, Gates plunged into an extended and emotional tirade, railing at the DOJ, castigating the judge, bemoaning the sheer irrationality of what had befallen him and his company. Everyone in the room was familiar with Gates's outbursts, which were an unfortunate but inescapable signature of his leadership style. But this was a different brand of diatribe—more stream-of-consciousness than usual, and far more personal. His voice quavered; his body quaked. And where Gates in full lather was normally condescending and sometimes cruel, now he was seized by unbridled self-pity. The DOJ was demonizing him. The press hated him. His rivals were conspiring to take him down. The political establishment was ganging up on him. His enemies were legion; his defenders, mute.

How had this happened? What could he do?

Gates's eyes reddened. "The whole thing is crashing in on me," he said. "It's all crashing in."

And with that, the richest man in the world fell silent, and began to cry.

Chapter 4

THINGS FALL APART

EVEN MIRED in the depths of despair, Bill Gates was no fool. As nasty a turn as his fortunes had taken in the past three months, he must have sensed, however inchoately, that his situation was about to get much worse. Before the consent-decree case, Gates's world had been a well-ordered place. Tempestuous, unpredictable, often brutal—no doubt. But it was a world Gates understood, and one he had mastered as thoroughly as anyone could. But now, with the repercussions of the dust-up with Jackson still sinking in, and with the DOJ reportedly edging closer to accusing the company of having violated the 100-year-old Sherman Antitrust Act, Microsoft stood at the threshold of a more complex and chaotic universe.

Complexity was Gates's strong suit. It was said by admirers and antagonists alike that he was endowed with a greater ability than perhaps any CEO in history not only to see several chess moves ahead but to do so on several chessboards simultaneously. Yet no matter how many chess games are being played, the same rules apply from board to board. Knowable rules. Fixed rules. The trouble for Gates and Microsoft was that the ordeal they now confronted was less like a chess match than a piece of improvisational theater, where the stage is full of actors armed with different scripts, motivations, and objectives. At times the players—Microsoft, the DOJ, the states, Silicon Valley, Judge Jackson, and the rest—would stay in character; at times not. At times they would read out well-rehearsed lines; at times they would extemporize wildly. Careening around the proscenium, this motley cast would send the Microsoft drama hurtling forward in ways that none of them expected, intended, or necessarily even desired.

For Microsoft, the most baffling of subplots was the one playing out in the realm of politics. Starting in 1997, a number of prominent Valley figures had begun building bridges to Washington, DC, in a manner unprecedented in the high-tech industry. The institutional form this outreach took was a bipartisan organization called TechNet, whose cochairmen were Netscape's Jim Barksdale and John Doerr, the venture capitalist who had funded not only Netscape but Sun, Intuit, @Home, and an array of other Microsoft rivals, and who was conspicuously tight with Al Gore. (So tight that the joke in the Valley went "Gore and Doerr in 2004.")

In Redmond, suspicions ran rampant that Barksdale, Doerr, and other TechNetters were using their newly minted access in the capital to lobby the administration and Congress to take on Microsoft. These suspicions weren't entirely unfounded. In the late summer of 1997, TechNet had arranged a trip to the Valley for the White House's then-deputy chief of staff, John Podesta, who met with top executives at firms such as Cisco, Adobe, Sybase, and Marimba. At many of those meetings, Podesta acknowledged, the subject of Microsoft was broached, "often obliquely—as in, concerns about technology control, concerns about the concentration of power," he said, but at times more bluntly—"as in, they're screwing us." And although Doerr and other TechNet officials swore to the skies that they never discussed Microsoft with Gore, a person connected to the group said that, on at least one occasion, a leading Silicon Valley figure spoke about it with Clinton. How did the president respond? "He expressed sympathy with our point of view," this person said. "But then, this was Clinton, so it could have been meaningless."

The effects of such lobbying were probably nil. Podesta and others in the White House with Silicon Valley ties denied ever talking about Microsoft substantively with Klein; and Klein denied that any communication between the DOJ and the White House occurred prior to the filing of either the consent-decree case or the broader Sherman Act suit. As for Clinton and Gore, it was plainly in their interest to steer clear of the Microsoft matter. Although Silicon Valley was a rich vein of campaign cash, the politics of pursuing Microsoft were highly fraught. "It's a no-winner," said Greg Simon, a senior Gore campaign official who previously served as the vice president's cyberpolicy guru. "People would say, 'Why are you going after them? Do you want to kill the goose that laid the golden egg?' " Simon's conclusion was unambiguous: "Politically, antitrust is a tar baby."

Even so, Microsoft wasn't wrong to fret that its foes were playing the influence game more adroitly than the company was. For if mining the muddy Clintonite middle yielded few tangible (or at least public) results, the Valley hit paydirt among those with more concrete ideologies. On the left there was Ralph Nader, whose anti-Microsoft summit in November 1997 featured Sun's Scott McNealy, Netscape's Roberta Katz, and Gary Reback as speakers. The event produced few surprises but a plethora of headlines.

More unexpected, and more influential, was the support the Valley managed to stir up on the right, much of it due to the labors of Mike Pettit. Pettit was an old Washington hand, a former top Senate aide to Bob Dole who had lobbied for Netscape in 1996 and 1997. In February 1998, he took over as the head of ProComp, the anti-Microsoft outfit funded initially by Sun, Netscape, and Sabre (and later by Oracle and others). Pettit was tireless and unusually—startlingly—bereft of ego. In short order, he put Dole on the ProComp payroll. He made inroads among Republicans on the Hill and among the conservative think tanks around Washington. And he proposed a slightly nutty idea: why not try to enlist Robert Bork to the cause?

Bork, the controversial conservative jurist whose nomination to the Supreme Court had caused such commotion in the summer of 1987, was one of the reigning lords of antitrust. His 1978 book, *The Antitrust Paradox,* was a sacred text for Chicago School economists and a generation of right-leaning judges who were named to the bench by Richard Nixon and Ronald Reagan, because of its potent arguments that antitrust enforcement was justified only in the rarest of cases. Microsoft would later dismiss Bork as having sold out his principles to become a hired gun for Netscape and ProComp. "I don't know if he was bought or if he's just tired, but he's making crappy arguments," said the Microsoft advisor Charles F. "Rick" Rule, who had held Klein's job at the DOJ under Reagan and Bush. "It's sad."

Rule failed to mention that Microsoft had also attempted to purchase Bork's services, and, at first, had seemed likely to get them. Bork was initially skeptical of Netscape's complaint—until he took a gander at the first Netscape white paper. There he found that Susan Creighton had drawn a comparison between Microsoft's actions against Netscape and those at issue in a 1951 Supreme Court case known as *Lorain Journal*. In the case, a local newspaper with a monopoly on advertising found itself facing a new technology—radio, a "partial substitute" that threatened the paper's monopoly—and sought to "destroy and eliminate" it by refusing ads from any advertiser doing business with the radio station. When Creighton discovered *Lorain Journal,* she knew she'd hit the jackpot, and not just because the Court had ruled that the newspaper had violated the Sherman Act or because the case seemed so apt. What thrilled Creighton most was where she had found *Lorain Journal*: in *The Antitrust Paradox,* cited approvingly by Bork. "I thought the analogy was perfect, and if I was right, we had the god of the Chicago School on our side," she said. "I dreamed about showing it to him someday and seeing if the light bulb went off."

It did. Presented with the white paper by Pettit and Netscape's Christine Varney, Bork gazed from his book to Creighton's and back again, then peered up over his half-glasses and said, "You're right, I wrote this. It applies. Perfectly." In March 1998, Bork officially joined the anti-Microsoft brigade.

Microsoft was stung, knowing that Bork's support would lend their enemies' cause instant intellectual credibility. Naturally, the company would hire its own bevy of Washington heavies. But among the relatively few executives in Redmond with a background in politics, Silicon Valley's success in nailing down support at both ends of the political spectrum was troubling. As one executive put it, "If Ralph Nader and Bob Bork agree about Microsoft, my God, there really is no political risk in going after us."

Enter Orrin Hatch. In February, Hatch announced that he was planning to hold a hearing on Microsoft—and to ask Bill Gates to attend. The idea belonged to Mike Hirshland, who was quickly becoming one of the capital's most avid, effective, and stealthy Microsoft hawks. Back in November, Hirshland had orchestrated a hearing on competition in the software industry that had generated little heat but some interesting information. Since then, the young lawyer had been digging further into the company's doings and had become convinced beyond doubt that there was a credible and winnable Sherman Act case waiting to be brought. Hirshland saw himself as a goad to the DOJ, and it was in that context that he went to Hatch and proposed inviting Gates to testify, along with several of Microsoft's most outspoken rivals.

To no small degree, Hirshland functioned as Hatch's frontal lobe when it came to the question of Microsoft, but the Mormon senator happened to dislike the company for reasons of his own as well. For years Hatch had heard tales of Microsoft's alleged dirty deeds against Utah-based tech firms like Novell and Caldera. If this wasn't reason enough to favor Hirshland's scheme, Hatch knew that, if Gates actually showed, the hearing was bound to win adulation from Silicon Valley and a copious quantity of TV time— and thus to feed Hatch's twin joneses, for campaign cash and national publicity. But Hatch also knew that such a high-wattage showdown could easily backfire. "I only want to do this if we know we can win," Hatch said to Hirshland, who assured him that it would be a slam dunk.

As the hearing date approached, Hatch told Hirshland that he wanted to bend over backward to ensure that the hearing was free of even the faintest hint of unfairness. So when Microsoft's CEO told the senator that he refused to testify alongside only Barksdale and McNealy, as Hirshland had originally suggested, Hatch readily acceded to the condition Gates attached to his appearance: that two of his handpicked allies—Michael Dell of Dell Computer and Doug Burgum of Great Plains Software—be added to the witness list. Moreover, the senator set aside a full hour for a briefing with Gates the day before the hearing, despite Hatch's normal practice of never—ever—allotting more than 20 minutes for any meeting.

On the drizzly Monday afternoon of March 2, Gates arrived with an entourage of nearly a dozen at Hatch's first-floor office in the Russell Senate Office Building, the decor of which was classic early-modern senatorial drab—blue carpet, dark wood, flag in the corner. Hatch was on the Senate floor, casting a vote, but soon he strode in and apologized for being tardy. Gates stared at the clock on the wall, turned to the chairman of the Senate Judiciary Committee, and said coolly, "Well, given that we're starting 15 minutes late and I'm only going to have 45 minutes now, we should get right to it."

Hatch, thunderstruck, said nothing.

Things went downhill from there. When Gates told Hatch that the DOJ was trying to force Microsoft to remove IE from Windows, Hirshland piped up and said that Microsoft's CEO was mischaracterizing the government's position. Whipping around, Gates snapped, "You're wrong. You don't know what you're talking about." When Gates demanded to see a summary of the questions he might be asked, Hirshland handed him a list of broad categories. Pointing to one topic, Gates wailed, "If you ask about that, this will be a kangaroo court!" Then Gates inquired about the seating arrangement for the hearing. When he was told he'd be seated between Barksdale and McNealy, Gates leapt to his feet and exploded, "No! No! No! If you put me between them, I will not appear at this hearing!"

Hatch, by now more amused than annoyed, leaned back and said, "OK, OK, we'll put you on one end of the table and we'll let you speak first. Happy?"

Compared with that prelude, the hearing itself was a bit of a letdown. Hundreds of gawkers lined up outside to catch a glimpse of Gates, who was decked out like a kid for a wedding in a suit and tie and proper leather shoes, his hair freshly cut and plastered down. Gates's handlers had studiously prepared him, putting him through mock hearings in which a Microsoft lawyer posed as Hatch and two Microsoft executives played McNealy and Barksdale. Even so, Gates's performance ranged from passable to poor. He was often evasive and, worse, failed to conceal it. He repeatedly contended that Microsoft was not a monopoly, a statement that met with pervasive skepticism. Only in the hearing's final minutes did an actual moment of drama arise, when a dogged (and well-briefed) Hatch was able to extract from Gates an admission that Microsoft's contracts with Internet content companies barred them from promoting Netscape's browser.

To many observers, especially those unacquainted with the inscrutable kabuki that passes for communication inside the Beltway, Hatch's convocation seemed to have accomplished little or nothing. Long on spectacle, short on substance, the skeptics said. And, anyway, Microsoft's legal fate rested not in the hands of Congress but in those of the DOJ and the courts.

Yet Joel Klein was not a man to embark on a crusade against Microsoft without first holding one wet finger in the air to gauge the political winds. And he was enough of a Washington veteran to understand that waging a case of this magnitude would be infinitely easier with the blessing, however tacit, of Capitol Hill. For that, Klein looked to Hatch, who had been his most valuable ally in his confirmation struggle. His gaze was well-directed. Hatch and Hirshland were indeed trying to send Klein a message about the mood on the Hill, and, in the process, to stiffen his spine. The message required no subtle deciphering: in a four-hour hearing, not a single member of the Senate Judiciary Committee had offered a serious defense of Microsoft—or launched any kind of preemptive attack on the DOJ.

"I knew there was political support for taking on Microsoft," Klein said a few weeks afterward. "That was not a shock to me. But the hearing provided a real sense of comfort. The politics of this thing are becoming clearer. Microsoft goes up to the Hill and says they don't have a monopoly, and people just say, 'That's silly.' "

To other politicos, silly was an understatement. Jeff Eisenach, the head of the Progress & Freedom Foundation, the think tank once known as Newt Gingrich's braintrust, said at the time, "Gates's performance didn't reflect petty arrogance; it reflected gross arrogance. It's the reason why Microsoft has no constituency in Washington right now, apart from a couple of extremists at the CATO Institute and some Austrian economists at some second-rate universities." Eisenach shook his head. "When Gates walked out of that hearing, he was a lot closer to a broad Sherman Act case than when he walked in. When you're the richest man in the world and not a single senator speaks up on your behalf, you know you've got problems."

THE HATCH hearing may have been a day in purgatory for Gates, but for his critics on the panel it was a day at the circus: the media circus. Barksdale had a ball. Silver-haired and Southern-fried, with courtly manners and a hint of hambone, Netscape's CEO seemed distinctly senatorial himself. He began his opening remarks by turning to the gallery and asking, in his best Mississippi drawl, how many people in the room had a PC. Maybe three-quarters of them raised their hands.

Barksdale asked, "How many of you use a PC without Microsoft's operating system?"

The hands all fell.

"Gentlemen, that's a monopoly."

McNealy, by contrast, seemed a touch nervous. He delivered his opening statement like a man with someplace else to be—which, it so happened, he was. Two-thirds of the way through the hearing, he committed a thumping faux pas by getting up abruptly and excusing himself so he could head up to New York for a business meeting. Before he left, however, McNealy snapped off a winner of his own, quipping that "the only thing I'd rather own than Windows is English . . . because then I could charge you $249 for the right to speak English, and I could charge you an upgrade fee when I add new letters—like N and T."

Even before the Senate shindig, Barksdale and McNealy had emerged as the public faces of the anti-Microsoft movement. (Larry Ellison was perhaps the Valley's loudest Gates-basher, but his inconstancy and clownish self-absorption had rendered him a plausible public face for nothing except playboyhood.) Netscape and Sun were loosely but indisputably aligned, despite the feuds that flared sporadically between their employees. Sun was a hardware firm that dabbled in software, and it was considerably larger and more established than its ally, with $8.6 billion in sales in 1997 compared with Netscape's $533 million. But when it came to the legal and political campaign against Microsoft, Netscape had always been the senior partner, both in front of the camera and backstage. It was Netscape's bid to topple the ogre—bold, romantic, inspiring, doomed—that had captured the public's imagination in a way Sun, even with Java, never could. It was Netscape that was Microsoft's main victim. And it was Netscape, with its white papers and the indefatigable lobbying efforts of Reback and Creighton, that had finally surmounted the DOJ's inertia and got things cooking in the courts.

Then, on the first working day of January 1998, Netscape announced it had badly missed its fourth-quarter earnings estimates; ultimately, it would report an $88 million loss and fire 400 of its 3,200 employees. At that moment, things changed. Nobody put out a press release saying so, but Netscape went up for sale that day. (The first suitor Barksdale entertained, later in January, was in fact McNealy, who craved Netscape's enterprise software but had less than zero interest in its Web portal, thus making a deal impossible.) While Netscape would remain forever the poster child of the Microsoft case—imagine Marc Andreessen's picture on the side of a milk carton—the pioneering start-up was no longer the brains or the heart of the anti-Microsoft coalition. Sun was.

Although McNealy had a reputation as Gates's most caustic and unrestrained critic—aside from Reback, that is—he assumed the mantle of leadership skittishly. Sun's CEO was one of the four men who launched the company back in 1982, and he had been running the place since 1984. He was simultaneously one of the most straightforward and most enigmatic chief executives in America. In his mid-forties, McNealy had a public persona of a laid-back, wisecracking, superannuated frat boy—"Huck Finn goes to business school," as one of Sun's top executives put it. Yet in private he displayed a volcanic temper and competitive impulses that matched Gates's in purity and extremity. He had formidable brainpower but didn't read books, and enjoyed bragging about the extent of his illiteracy. He jealously guarded his privacy but relished the limelight. And despite having cultivated an image as a brash, high-sticking, trash-talking corporate rebel, inside Sun his management style had always been cautious and conflict-averse to the point of phobia. He was known to be incapable of firing anyone (for that deed he used surrogates) and rarely made decisions without first achieving consensus on his senior staff. "His demeanor is radical," Mike Morris, Sun's general counsel, remarked. "But his instincts are conservative."

Those instincts were forever at odds with McNealy's antipathy for Microsoft, which was real and deep and unforgiving. As Sun had transformed itself from an obscure workstation maker into a leading manufacturer of high-end servers, competing with giants such as IBM and HP, some of McNealy's lieutenants, and especially his number two, Ed Zander, had encouraged him to mute his Microsoft attacks. We need détente with Redmond, he was told; our customers are begging for it. In October, after agreeing to deliver the keynote address at the Nader conference in Washington, McNealy took so much flak from Zander and others that he backed out. Then he stepped back in. Then out again. At last, McNealy said he would go if Nader found another CEO to speak in addition to him. With the help of a sympathetic and plugged-in venture capitalist in the Valley, Nader persuaded Sybase's then-CEO Mitchell Kertzman to appear via satellite, which proved to be sufficient to satisfy McNealy.

Sun's boss was also uncomfortable with lobbying the government, even on Microsoft, because he didn't believe in it—the government, that is. "Washington, DC, is my least favorite town in the world," he told me at one point. "I see all these unbelievable monuments to government, agencies that have no reason for being on the planet—the Department of Agriculture, Transportation, FEMA, Health, Education, Commerce—all these huge erections of brick and mortar with their masses of people running around redistributing wealth. The whole thing drives me absolutely into a freaking funk."

I noted that McNealy hadn't included the DOJ in his list of huge erections. He smiled. I asked what he thought the Feds should do about Microsoft. "Shut down some of the bullshit the government is spending money on and use it to buy all the Microsoft stock. Then put all their intellectual property in the public domain. Free Windows for everyone! Then we could just bronze Gates, turn him into a statue, and stick him in front of the Commerce Department."

Had McNealy's legal theories been all that Sun brought to the anti-Microsoft movement, Redmond could have rested easy. But the company brought Mike Morris, too. A smallish man with a round belly, a brown beard, and pudding-bowl bangs across his forehead, Morris had been Sun's chief lawyer since 1987. Like McNealy, he was a Michigan native, but they had grown up on decidedly different sides of the tracks—McNealy in posh Bloomfield Hills, as the son of a top-tier auto-industry executive, Morris in the sticks, as the son of a tool-and-die maker. And that was the least of the differences between them. Where McNealy was a blunderbuss when it came to politics, and a libertarian whose taste in presidential candidates ran to Steve Forbes, Morris was a capital-L liberal with the cagey instincts of a natural political consultant. Where McNealy was screamingly heterosexual, Morris was openly gay. And where McNealy shied away from conflict and confrontation, Morris gloried in it, especially when his adversary was Microsoft. It was Morris who had pushed McNealy to file the Java lawsuit in October 1997. After claiming a victory there, Morris persuaded his boss to file another Java suit, this one more radical, in that it asked the court to order Microsoft to make changes in

Windows. In the midst of a furious internal debate over filing the second suit, Ed Zander accused Morris of being a "fanatic."

"I'm not a fanatic, I'm just realistic," Morris said angrily. "We've got our boots on their throats. The right thing to do is to press until they stop breathing. If you're going to strike at the king, you better cut his head off."

Decapitating Microsoft was on Morris's mind again when, a few days into 1998, he picked up the phone and called Joel Klein. For the past nine months, Morris had been in contact with Klein as part of a three-way effort to nudge the government toward a case against Microsoft. His partners in the triad were Netscape's Roberta Katz and Sabre's counsel, Andy Steinberg. Together they'd founded ProComp; lobbied the DOJ; assisted Mike Hirshland in his inquiries; told their tale in concert—from the multiple, harmonious viewpoints of a systems company, a software company, and a content company—to anyone who would listen; and urged wary Silicon Valley bigwigs to talk in confidence to the DOJ. Now Morris was plotting a solo mission: to put together a sort of private blue-ribbon commission of nationally renowned antitrust lawyers and economists, have them draw up an outline of the kind of Sherman Act case that would make sense for the DOJ to file, including a discussion of possible remedies, and then present the whole thing to Klein and his people.

Might the DOJ find that helpful? Morris asked the assistant attorney general.

Sure we would, Klein replied.

So began a project that would span three months and consume $3 million of Sun's money: "Project Sherman." As Morris intended, Project Sherman drew together a superstar group of antitrust authorities, including the famed Houston litigator Harry Reasoner; University of Chicago economist Dennis Carlton and several of his colleagues from the economic consulting firm Lexecon; Arnold & Porter chairman and prominent Washington attorney Michael Sohn; Stanford economist Garth Saloner; and former FTC general counsel Kevin Arquit, who handled Sun's antitrust work in Washington. In choosing his experts, Morris took care to select people with impeccable credentials—mainstream credentials, establishment credentials—the kind of people who spoke Klein's language, the kind who might come across as reasonably objective despite the fact that Sun was paying them $600 to $700 an hour. The political sensitivity of the project was, needless to say, extremely high, for here was one of Microsoft's most ardent competitors bankrolling a costly endeavor to influence the DOJ—an endeavor undertaken with the department's encouragement. And so it was conducted in utmost secrecy. Apart from McNealy, Morris informed almost no one at Sun, and everyone involved was sworn to strict confidentiality. When asked about his role in the project, one of the participants said furtively, "I haven't even told my wife about this."

From mid-January to mid-April, the Project Sherman crew met every two weeks, usually at the O'Hare Hilton in Chicago. At first, the meetings were contentious. For one thing, "There was an awful lot of ego in that room," one person said. "An awful lot of grandstanding." For another, the group quickly divided into factions: lawyers and economists; tech-savvy and tech-challenged; Washington insiders and Washington outsiders. "We had these people who claimed to know Joel well," recalled one participant. "They'd say all the time, 'Let me tell you, I know Joel, and Joel will never go for that.'" The problem was especially nettlesome when it came to the question of remedies. One economist recalled, "The Washington people kept arguing for conduct remedies because they were so sure Joel would never agree to a structural remedy." He laughed. "Boy, I guess they must be feeling pretty dumb now."

There was another debilitating split within the group. Among those from the Valley, the idea that Microsoft's monopoly and its predatory practices had chilled innovation and distorted investment was taken for granted; it was a given. But for people like Reasoner, Carlton, and Sohn—the big guns, whom Morris intended to wheel out in front of Klein—it was speculation garnished with hearsay. Reasoner kept asking, "Where the hell is the evidence?"

Morris's plan was to bring the Project Sherman gang to the Valley and expose them firsthand to Microsoft's influence. He turned to Gary Reback, asking him to arrange a series of hush-hush meetings with industry figures who could address the question with authority. Nothing gave Reback more kicks than a covert operation where he was pulling the strings. He told Morris, "I'll call in all my chits." (Morris: "If Gary called in all his chits every time he's said he's calling in all his chits, he'd running one huge chit deficit by now.") Within days, Reback had assembled a Murderer's Row of Valley executives, financiers, and technologists who would parade before Morris's group during a single daylong session. Reback told his witnesses that the meeting was important and that it might help influence the DOJ, but he told them little else; not the names of the economists and lawyers they'd be addressing, or who their fellow witnesses would be, or the identity of the meeting's sponsor. To keep them from running into one another at Wilson Sonsini's offices, he instructed them to enter and exit through different lobbies.

The tutorial the Project Shermanites received on the appointed late-March day was wide-ranging, and, according to several people who attended, they reacted to parts of it with shock and amazement. They heard from Eric Schmidt, the CEO of Novell, about the vulnerability of being a firm that both competes with, and is reliant on, Microsoft software. They heard from the

Apple software wizard Avie Tevanian about why conduct remedies like opening up Microsoft's APIs wouldn't accomplish anything. They heard from Sun's Bill Joy (who, because of the secrecy surrounding the meeting, was totally unaware that his own company was paying for it) about why Tevanian was right, but why splitting Microsoft into three identical firms, the so-called Baby Bills solution, might be worse: "I keep thinking of 'The Sorcerer's Apprentice,'" Joy said. They heard from John Doerr about Microsoft's recent habit of gathering together the Valley's venture capitalists and offering "helpful" guidance and suggestions about which technologies were advisable to invest in and which might be best left to Redmond. "My firm's policy is never to back a venture that competes directly with Microsoft," Doerr said. "Only damned fools stand in the way of oncoming trains."

And they heard from Jim Clark. "When I left Silicon Graphics I had a net worth of $16 million and I invested $5 million to start Netscape," Clark said. "Microsoft has practically killed Netscape. I'll never invest in another thing to compete with them. I'll never touch another market that has anything remotely to do with Microsoft's path. And if I'd known four years ago what I know now—that Microsoft would destroy us and that the government wouldn't do anything about it for three fucking years—I never would've started Netscape in the first place."

A few weeks later, after a mad scramble to reach their conclusions and complete a presentation, Morris and a select subset of his experts (big guns plus Saloner; no Reback) flew out to Washington for their audience with the DOJ. It was now the middle of April. Four months had passed since the consent-decree case had climaxed, and Morris knew little more about where the DOJ's investigation stood than what he read in the papers. Certainly the trustbusters seemed eager to see him: Klein had called twice to try to move up the date of the presentation. And when Morris arrived at the DOJ, he found his squad was playing to a packed house. Klein, Melamed, Rubinfeld, Malone, and David Boies were there, along with a swarm of junior antitrust-division staffers, all crowded into the conference room next to Klein's office.

Taking seats across the table from Klein and his deputies, Morris's team proceeded to outline the case they believed the DOJ should file. Just as the Netscape white papers had argued, the core of that case was illegal monopoly maintenance and monopoly extension—a violation of Section 2 of the Sherman Act. For years, Microsoft had leveraged its power over the desktop to invade adjacent markets, from productivity applications to server operating systems. Sometimes those markets were tremendously valuable in their own right; Office alone raked in billions each year for Gates's company, and Microsoft's next target—the server space in which Sun was a leader—was even richer. Other times, the market itself was worth next to nothing in terms of dollars and cents, but controlling it was essential to preserving Microsoft's dominance on the desktop. Browsers were one example of this. But Java was an equally compelling one. By letting programmers write software that would run on any OS, Java threatened to render Windows irrelevant, if not obsolete. Microsoft's response had been to license Java from Sun and then, Sun claimed, to violate that license by creating a Windows-only variant of the technology in an attempt to subvert its cross-platform purpose. With both Java and the browser, as Saloner put it later, Microsoft's philosophy was the same: "We will embrace it, we will make it ours, we will apply it to our operating system, and we will kill it. We will do what we must to protect the mothership—the OS."

The Sun presentation ran for nearly four hours. Deploying his experts to make most of the arguments—Reasoner and Sohn on the law, Carlton on the economics—Morris tried to anticipate and shoot down Microsoft's defenses. In particular, the team addressed the question of harm, of who'd been hurt by Microsoft's actions. After all, the company would say, consumers are happy; prices are falling; high tech is thriving; so is Sun, by the way. What that picture left out, however, was the damage to innovation—the products left undeveloped, the areas of technology left unexplored. For example, there was almost no R&D on operating systems anymore. What did that imply for the future of technology? And how long could innovation continue to flourish in an industry suffused with fear?

"I went out to Silicon Valley," Mike Sohn told Klein and his team. "In all my years practicing antitrust law, I have never seen such powerful people so scared. It utterly amazed me."

At the end of the afternoon, the talk turned to remedies, and Dennis Carlton took the floor. In a way, Carlton was the least likely, and thus the most impressive, member of the Sun team. One of the best-regarded economists in the country, he was also a classic conservative straight out of the Chicago School: suspicious of plaintiffs, friendly to business, inherently skeptical of government intervention in general and of antitrust enforcement in particular. All of which was why Morris had worked doggedly to recruit him in the first place.

Throughout the day, Carlton had spoken with calm conviction about the economics of the case, about monopoly maintenance, market power, and Microsoft's predation. Now, with the DOJ officials hanging on every word, Carlton did what had once been nearly unthinkable. First, he laid out a range of conduct remedies (contract restrictions, technical requirements) and methodically described the pros and cons of each, in every case listing more cons than pros. Then, without the slightest hesitation, he presented the case for a structural remedy—not a full-blown breakup of Microsoft, but a scheme that would force the firm to license all its intellectual property to some number of third parties, giving birth to a set of clone companies that would create competition in the markets for operating systems and applications.

Garth Saloner knew it was coming, but even he found it a powerful moment. "This is not one of us Silicon Valley loonies saying this," Saloner later observed. "This isn't Gary Reback. This isn't Roberta Katz. This isn't Garth Saloner. This is Dennis Carlton. Things have moved. The world has changed. If you're Joel Klein or Dan Rubinfeld, I would think you'd take comfort in that."

Mike Morris had no illusions that Klein and his colleagues would swallow the case his team put forward—let alone the remedy—whole. Instead he was trying, as he explained it, to accomplish something less ambitious but equally valuable: "to give them a sense that this wasn't a wild-goose chase, that this was a good case, a real case."

As the meeting drew to a close, it was impossible to know if the effort had succeeded. For several hours, the DOJ officials had adopted what one participant described as a "highway-patrol demeanor": professional, poker-faced, pristinely neutral. They had asked countless questions but given nothing away.

But many months later, Dan Rubinfeld reflected on the Sun presentation in a way that would have given Morris no small measure of satisfaction. "It was memorable. It was impressive. It told us some things that we did not know," Rubinfeld said. "But mostly, and this can't be underestimated, it reinforced in our minds that what we were doing wasn't crazy."

■ ■ ■

WHAT THE DOJ was doing was girding for war. By mid-April, Klein had persuaded David Boies to sign on as the antitrust division's "special trial counsel" for about one-fifteenth of his customary $600-an-hour fee. ("It didn't take a lot of persuading," Klein recalled. "About a half a second after I asked, he said, 'When do I start?' ") Klein also brought another pivotal player into his inner circle: Jeffrey Blattner. A former chief counsel to Senator Edward Kennedy's staff on the Senate Judiciary Committee, Blattner had made his reputation in Washington as a sharp operator during the battle to keep Robert Bork off the Supreme Court. His new title was Special Counsel for Information Technology, but his de facto role was chief of staff for the Microsoft case, with duties that would include stroking the Hill, spinning the press, and plugging any (unwanted) leaks from within the division.

In short, all the smoke signals wafting out of the DOJ indicated that Klein was on the verge of filing a broad Sherman Act suit. The only questions were: How broad? And to what end?

To find out, I arranged to meet Klein on the Saturday morning after the Sun presentation. It was a brilliant spring day, with Washington aswirl in cherry blossoms and dogwood. Over the next two years, Klein and I would have nearly a dozen of these discussions. The setting was always the same: Klein's fourth-floor corner office, where he would sit in a high-backed leather chair, dressed usually in a dark suit and tie, and talk for an hour or two about the strategy, tactics, and legal principles at stake in a case he believed would help set the rules of competition for the digital age. He spoke quickly, quietly, candidly, and not without humor, in a voice still tinged with the accents of Astoria and Bensonhurst, where he'd grown up.

"I think we're at decision-making time," Klein began, pointing out that the introduction of Windows 98 was only a few weeks away. After months of concentrated investigation, Klein was satisfied that he had sufficient evidence to level a number of charges against Microsoft: that its exclusive contracts with ISPs and content providers were anticompetitive; that its contracts with OEMs placing "first-screen" restrictions on how they could modify the Windows desktop and boot-up sequence were illegal; and that its integration of IE with Windows constituted an unlawful tying together of two separate products. In all this, Klein said, the company's motives were clear, and clearly predatory. "When you see document after document, from Gates on down, saying that Netscape could basically commoditize the operating system, that's important stuff," he said. "That's what was going on in the minds of these people when they say, Well, what we ought to do in response is go right at 'em and cut off their oxygen."

Klein felt confident that each of these tactics was a violation of Section 1 of the Sherman Act, which states: "Every contract, combination in the form of trust or otherwise, or conspiracy, in restraint of trade or commerce among the several States, or with foreign nations, is declared to be illegal." The question was whether to go further and accuse Microsoft of monopoly maintenance under Section 2. Section 2 says: "Every person who shall monopolize, or attempt to monopolize, or combine or conspire with any other person or persons to monopolize any part of the trade or commerce among the several States . . . shall be deemed guilty of a felony."

For all the exhortations of Netscape and Sun, monopoly maintenance was not a mainstream case to bring. And it wouldn't be a simple one to prove, especially given the products in question. To start with, explaining how the combination of Java and Netscape's browser, neither of which was a direct rival to Windows, nonetheless posed a threat to the OS would require the DOJ not only to elucidate the intricacies of software APIs but to do so in a vocabulary that Judge Jackson (who, having presided over the consent-decree case, would handle any related Sherman Act suit) could readily comprehend. No mean feat, that.

Inside the DOJ, a pitched debate was still being waged between those who preferred to keep it simple, to stick with a more traditional Section 1 case, and those angling hard for Section 2. Dan Rubinfeld was still among the most hawkish of the hawks, though now he was joined by the hard-line David Boies and Jeff Blattner. "Contrary to what a lot of other economists and lawyers in the division believed, I thought it would be perhaps easier to win a bigger case than a narrower one," Rubinfeld recalled. "What we had with Microsoft was a pattern of practices where the whole was greater than the sum of the parts." And although the majority of misdeeds the DOJ had nailed down so far—including the June 1995 meeting between Microsoft and Netscape—revolved around the browser, the investigation had begun to unearth evidence of Microsoft malfeasance involving other competitors. "We hadn't had time to flesh out the pattern of bad acts completely," Rubinfeld said. By filing a Section 2 claim, "we could put a legal place-holder in our complaint and try to fill it in later. If we could stand it up, the case would be broad. If we couldn't, it would be a browser case."

Klein said he was leaning toward making a Section 2 claim. "The browser is a big part of the story, but I'm also interested in what other products can be implicated in the same kind of squeeze," he told me. "If it weren't for the timing of Windows 98, we might be inclined to develop some of the other issues that are still being intensively investigated. Having said that, the fundamental structure of the case in terms of monopoly power, monopoly maintenance, monopoly expansion—if we file it that way—would be the kind of thing that would at least lend itself to extensions."

The scope of the case Klein was contemplating was sweeping, but the tone of his comments was in keeping with his character: cautious, temperate, carefully calibrated. For nine months, Klein had heard from every putative Microsoft victim in the known world. He'd heard tales of treachery, duplicity, and outright thuggery. He had watched as the mood in Washington turned decisively against Gates and his company. And yet, far from spoiling for a fight, he still seemed wary, ever so gun-shy. On the question of what sort of remedy he might seek, Klein expressed a preference for something "surgical." Did that mean he wasn't considering a breakup? "I think that's accurate—at least for now," he replied. "There are real costs that one has to be very cognizant of to breaking up a company like Microsoft." When I asked if he felt any sense of moral outrage over Microsoft's conduct, he blurted out, "No, no, no, no. This is not tobacco stuff, it really isn't. I don't think what they're doing has that sense of dishonesty and deception. On the merits of the issues, they have arguments that are legitimate. We at the Department of Justice do not have a monopoly on wisdom."

I asked Klein if he'd ever met Gates, and he said that he hadn't. Was he looking forward to that day?

"I don't know. People ask me this a lot. Maybe it reflects a blind spot. I mean, obviously there's something about meeting Bill Gates—though, as my kids would tell me, it's not as exciting as meeting some rock star. I feel weird, because I have the sense that everybody expects there's gonna be this great day. But I don't personalize this stuff. I really don't."

■ ■ ■

THE GREAT day arrived just two weeks later, when Gates and Neukom traveled from Seattle to Washington for a summit with Klein and his lieutenants. The Justice Department had put Microsoft on notice that it intended to file suit sometime before May 15, the Windows 98 ship date; at least a dozen state attorneys general were prepared to do the same. Now it was time to offer the prospective defendant a final opportunity to reach an accord outside of court—a meeting known inside the antitrust division as "last rites."

On the evening of May 5, the two camps convened in the offices of Sullivan & Cromwell, in an eighth-floor conference room with windows looking out on the Old Executive Office Building. On Microsoft's side of the table were Gates, Neukom, and a pair of S&C attorneys; on the DOJ's side were Klein, Boies, Blattner, and Melamed. Typically, when a company and the government get together in an effort to avert a massive lawsuit, the tenor of the discussions is all about give and take, with each side laboring, however misguided it thinks the other is, to find common ground. But Gates's approach "was more in the nature of a lecture—the world according to Gates—than a constructive dialogue," Klein said later. For the next two hours, Microsoft's CEO held forth—forcefully, passionately, often patronizingly—about the nature of the software business and the needs of his company. He asked no questions of the DOJ, and his answers to theirs took the form of prolonged soliloquies.

In the world according to Gates, the notion that Microsoft had a monopoly was ludicrous. "Give me any seat at the table—Java, OS/2, Linux—and I'd end up where I am," he proclaimed. "I could blow Microsoft away! I'd have programmers in India clone our APIs. If you were smart enough, you could do it." Asked if Netscape's browser was designed to compete with Windows, Gates shot back, "Not compete. Eliminate."

When the DOJ team tried to get Gates to address the full range of their concerns—the exclusive contracts, the first-screen restrictions—he repeatedly brushed them off, returning again and again to a single issue: integration. Klein recalled, "He made the argument in myriad different ways that the future of technology was through product integration; that he'd put billions of things into the operating system and he needed to be able to keep putting whatever he wanted into Windows. And if the government blocked that, it would basically kill his business. That was the clear top line, bottom line, and every line in between." What startled Klein was the personal terms in which Gates expressed these points. "It wasn't just, You're going to kill my business; it was, You're going to kill *me*. And clearly we, the government, were the instrument of this great personal affliction."

As David Boies sat quietly watching Gates give no quarter, he couldn't help thinking that the king of software was dangerously underestimating his adversary. From his decade-long stint in the trenches of the IBM case, Boies knew as well as anyone that the DOJ wasn't just another opponent; that it had "the same resources, the same imperatives, the same commitment" as any corporation, no matter how resolute. It was a point worth making, he told himself. So as the meeting drew to an end, Boies looked across the table at Gates and Neukom and asked if he could offer a word of advice.

"You know," Boies said, "once the United States government files suit against you, everything changes. People you thought you could trust turn against you. People you thought were your allies turn out to be enemies. Everyone is more willing to question you, to resist you. The whole world changes."

Gates and Neukom stared blankly back. "The government kept making these melodramatic statements," one of the Microsoft lawyers recalled. "They just didn't understand the fundamentals of our business. It was a bit like two ships passing in the night."

Initially, Klein felt the same way. But as he turned the meeting over in his mind afterward, he began to discern in the contours of Gates's intransigence what he thought were the faint outlines of a settlement. Microsoft seemed to be signaling that the first-screen limitations and restrictive contracts meant little to it. Maybe, if the company was willing to give significant ground on those issues, and if the DOJ showed flexibility on product integration, a deal could be done that would satisfy both parties.

For the next nine days, Klein and Neukom burned up the phone lines with proposals and counters. From the Microsoft side came a series of concessions to loosen the firm's grip on the first screen and give OEMs greater freedom over the Windows desktop. The company also offered a variety of ideas—a "browser folder," perhaps, or a "ballot screen" whereby users could choose between IE and Navigator—to create a more level playing field for Netscape. Indeed, at 1:30 A.M. on the Thursday that the DOJ was set to file suit, Gates himself phoned Klein at home to discuss whether Microsoft might agree to a "must-carry" provision wherein it would ship Netscape's browser with every copy of Windows. A few hours later, after another conversation with Neukom, Klein decided to delay launching the suit until the following Monday, so Microsoft and the DOJ could devote the weekend to face-to-face negotiations.

In Silicon Valley the sound that greeted the DOJ's announcement was the gnashing of high-tech teeth; in Washington, it was the low murmur of cynical assumptions being confirmed. What the Valley had long feared and the political class had long expected finally seemed to be coming to pass: at the eleventh hour, Joel Klein was caving. And although that judgment was rather too harsh, at its core there was a kernel of truth: Klein wanted a settlement and he wanted it badly.

The reasons were almost too numerous to count. In suing Microsoft, Klein would be taking on a company with unlimited resources and the best legal talent that money could buy, not to mention a PR operation populated by literally hundreds of foot-soldiers, strategists, and high-priced ad gurus. For all the tarnishing Gates's image had recently suffered, Microsoft's CEO remained an icon of the new economy. Even for a man more daring by nature than Klein, the political and legal risks of challenging Gates were daunting, the rewards uncertain. If Klein settled the case, he could declare victory and go home. The victory would be limited, but it would also be immediate—no small thing in an industry racing forward on Internet time. And it would avert a protracted lawsuit in which the government's prospects were decidedly dodgy. A month earlier, the DOJ and Microsoft had argued the appeal of the consent-decree case before a three-judge panel on the US Court of Appeals for the District of Columbia, and the judges had seemed markedly hostile to the government's position. As for the broader case the DOJ was about to unleash, the antitrust establishment (Mike Morris's experts notwithstanding) regarded it as a shot in the dark.

Even Boies had his doubts. "At that point, we didn't have all the evidence that we would subsequently get," he said later. "We had some evidence of Microsoft's broader conduct, but they denied that conduct. We had a lot of things we believed, but whether we could ultimately prove them or not was very uncertain. We had a judge who we thought was a good judge, but he was a careful judge, a very conservative judge. We knew he was going to make us prove every element of the offense. So we were in a situation where, if we could have achieved anything like a reasonable settlement, I think we would have jumped at it."

Dan Rubinfeld remembered thinking that Microsoft could have—should have—capitalized on the DOJ's eagerness to settle. "If I had been free to give them advice, that was the moment I would have said, 'Look, this is the time. Do a deal with us. You know me. You trust me. Really. Do it.'"

Instead, Neukom flew back to Washington, sat down with the DOJ and the states on a Friday afternoon, and played a brand of hardball that quickly brought the negotiations to a grinding halt. Not long into the first session, it seemed clear to the government that certain compromises Microsoft had already offered—in particular, ceding power over the desktop to OEMs—were now being yanked off the table. If that was so, there was not much to talk about. For Microsoft's part, one of its top attorneys said that the government's "basic attitude throughout was arms-folded, we-need-more, we-need-more. They made no counteroffers. We were not difficult or nonchalant. We tried our darnedest."

Late on Saturday morning, Neukom drafted a memo laying out Microsoft's stance (which included dropping its restrictive contracts, adopting the browser "ballot page," and not much else) and handed it to Jeff Blattner, who was leading the DOJ's negotiating team. Blattner could see that the talks were about to fall apart and suspected that Microsoft might leak the memo to the press. Pushing it back across the table, he said abruptly, "I don't negotiate from a list." Roughly translated, that meant sayonara.

■ ■ ■

IN RETROSPECT, Microsoft's failure to settle seems a colossal and inexplicable blunder. The retreat from its first-screen concessions was mysterious enough. (Had Neukom gotten ahead of Gates? Had Gates himself had a change of heart? Had the DOJ misunderstood the company's previous offers?) But even putting that aside, there were any number of other solutions at hand. In the consent-decree case, for example, Microsoft had agreed to offer OEMs two versions of Windows 95, one with IE visible, the other with it hidden; already it was clear that most of the OEMs were taking the version the company preferred. Had Gates proposed that the same arrangement be applied to Windows 98, the company would have sacrificed little in business terms and conceded nothing about its future right to integrate features into the operating system. Meanwhile, the government would have been hard-pressed to spurn the offer, as its officials would later acknowledge. Yet Gates, Neukom, and the rest of the Microsoft legal team all said that this entirely obvious idea was never entertained by the company; and that the question was irrelevant anyway because the DOJ would never have accepted anything less than forcing Microsoft to carry Netscape's browser.

There was, however, an alternative explanation: that despite the Sturm und Drang of those 10 days in May, Microsoft's real aim in the settlement negotiations was something other than settlement. "It was a fishing expedition," Christine Varney opined. "Microsoft wanted to find out what was in the case. When you're a litigant, you want to know as much as possible about what you're facing—if there's some smoking gun that you don't know about. So you find out, then you recalibrate and decide whether to settle or not."

What Microsoft found out—or thought it found out—was that the suit the DOJ intended to bring wasn't nearly as sweeping as the company had feared. To Microsoft's lawyers, it sounded like a browser case, a tying case, and tying was the legal ground on which they believed that their standing was firmest. "They thought, 'This is going to be a narrow case, so let's fight it,' " Boies said. " 'If we lose, we lose a narrow issue. We can afford to fight this case and lose.' " He went on, "Also, remember that Microsoft had been fighting with the government in one way or another for almost 10 years. And every time, they'd managed to come out really well. I think they thought they were smarter than we were. I think they thought they knew more than we did. And both of those things may very well have been true. But I think they underestimated our ability and willingness to learn."

Microsoft wasn't alone in its view that the government's case was a narrow one. When the DOJ and a grand total of 20 state attorneys general filed suit on May 18, the Monday after the settlement talks collapsed, the complaint charged Microsoft with four counts of violating the Sherman Act: exclusive dealing and unlawful tying under Section 1; monopoly maintenance in the OS market and attempted monopolization of the browser market under Section 2. Yet the narrative that Klein spun around the case painted Netscape as its hero and victim, and the short-term remedy the DOJ was seeking was glaringly Netscape-centric: a preliminary injunction forcing Microsoft either to offer a version of Windows 98 without IE or to bundle Navigator with the OS as well. Netscape was thrilled: it certainly looked like a browser case to Jim Barksdale. Sun was disconsolate: it looked like a browser case to Mike Morris, too. And the rest of the Valley rolled its eyes: didn't the government realize that the browser war was over? "If they'd done two years ago what they did today, it might have been useful," Reback groaned from a New York phone booth. "It's been a long haul to get this far. It's going to be a long march to get where we need to be. And some of us are getting awfully tired."

Some of them were worse off than that. Since the early days of Reback's efforts, no one in government had been a more steadfast ally than Mark Tobey. The assistant attorney general from Texas had started the ball rolling with his Netscape depositions and then lobbied furiously to create a groundswell among the states. But a few days before the Sherman Act case was filed, Texas had been forced to withdraw its support, under pressure from the state's computermaking kingpins, Compaq and Dell. Because both companies were dependent on Microsoft, the widespread assumption was that they were acting on orders from Redmond. Tobey told Reback, "I never dreamed they'd be able to shut me down entirely."

Then came another blow to the anti-Microsoft movement, a development that plunged the DOJ into sudden despair. On June 23, the federal Appeals Court issued its ruling in the consent-decree case. Striking down Judge Jackson's preliminary injunction, the Appeals Court found that he had "erred procedurally," by not giving Microsoft a chance to contest the injunction, and "substantively," by misreading the law on tying. "Antitrust scholars have long recognized the undesirability of having courts oversee product design, and any dampening of technological innovation would be at cross-purposes with antitrust law," the Court's opinion read. "We suggest here only that the limited competence of courts to evaluate high tech product designs and the high cost of error should make them wary of second-guessing the claimed benefits of a particular design decision."

In Microsoft's eyes, it was an overwhelming victory. All along, Bill Neukom and his team had assured Gates that the law was solidly on Microsoft's side—and now here was the proof in black and white. They had told him that the heart of the government's case was tying—and now here was an opinion suggesting, in essence, that the DOJ's tying claims were doomed. On hearing the news, Neukom crowed to reporters, "We view this very much as a vindication of our business practices and legal strategy." And for once, his optimism seemed in sync with reality.

The next morning, Neukom's boss picked up *The New York Times* and read that even Klein's sympathizers shared Microsoft's assessment of the Appeals Court's ruling. "This cuts the legs out from under the Justice Department on their new case," the former DOJ antitrust official Robert Litan, a Democratic appointee who had served under Anne Bingaman, was quoted as saying. "It's potentially devastating."

For the first time in months, reading the *Times* made Bill Gates smile.

DAVID BOIES was smiling too, though it made his associates think him deranged. By common consensus, Boies was the most brilliant litigator of his generation. Graduating second in his class from Yale Law School, he had spent 30 years with the white-shoe New York firm Cravath, Swaine & Moore before setting up his own shop in 1997. Over the years, Boies had represented a vast assortment of splashy clients against an array of even splashier opponents. In addition to his antitrust work for IBM, he had defended CBS against a takeover bid by Ted Turner and a libel suit by General William Westmoreland. He had helped Texaco fight off the corporate raider Carl Icahn and helped Westinghouse take on Philippine president Corazon Aquino. On behalf of George Steinbrenner, he'd sued Major League Baseball; on behalf of the government, he'd sued Michael Milken. He rarely lost at trial and had never had a victory overturned on appeal.

In his mid-fifties, Boies had thinning brown hair, a flat Midwestern twang in his voice, and a downmarket demeanor (Lands' End suits worn with blue knit ties he bought by the bagful) that belied an annual paycheck of more than $2 million. His courtroom manner was casual and conversational, which tended to lull his adversaries into a fatal haze of complacency. His memory was borderline photographic; his competitiveness, modestly terrifying. To a colleague at Cravath he once uttered the words that will surely be his epitaph: "Would you rather sleep or win?"

Boies got hold of a copy of the Appeals Court decision just before boarding a flight from New York to San Francisco. By the time the plane landed, he was certain that, far from being a death knell, the opinion actually worked to the DOJ's advantage. "It helped in three ways," he later observed. First, although the court was plainly on Microsoft's side, it made no bones about the fact that the company had a monopoly. Second, Boies said, when it came to tying, "the court said that if you can prove that they don't need the tie to achieve the benefits, then that's just bolting two products together, and that violates the tying laws." Third, he went on, "the court said that if you can prove that they did it not for efficiency purposes but for anticompetitive purposes, that trumps everything. In other words, the court was adopting an intent standard, and, given the Microsoft documents we had in hand, that was a standard I thought we could meet."

The Appeals Court had effectively provided Boies with a kind of road map, a guide for framing his arguments on product integration. At the same time, what the court said didn't touch the DOJ's Section 2 claims—claims that Boies now believed it was essential for the government to beef up before the trail began. But more than all that, the ruling gave Boies an overarching sense of confidence about the case in general. "Even in a decision that was really quite pro-Microsoft, there was no hint that the court was saying, 'The antitrust laws don't apply here; we're going to give the software industry or Microsoft a free pass,' " he noted. "And once I knew they didn't get a free pass, I knew we could prove an antitrust violation."

To do that, however, and especially to flesh out a powerful case of monopoly maintenance, Boies would need witnesses—strong and credible ones. And, unfortunately, the DOJ would have precious little time to round them up. When the government filed suit, both sides had assumed that Judge Jackson would hold a quick hearing on the DOJ's request for a preliminary injunction and then schedule a full trial to start perhaps a year later. But apparently Jackson had other ideas. In a surprise maneuver, he decided to put aside any preliminary hearing and move directly to trial—and soon, setting a date to commence in early September. If Jackson had his way, *US v. Microsoft* would be short and sweet. To ensure that it was, he adopted an unusual procedure limiting each side to 12 witnesses, all of whom would deliver their direct testimony not on the stand but in writing, with courtroom hours being reserved strictly for cross-examination.

The accelerated schedule set the DOJ a formidable task. In the course of their investigation, the government had accumulated a multitude of leads regarding instances of Microsoftian misconduct. Now Klein and his team had the summer months to chase down those allegations, establish their veracity, and then persuade a reasonable number of the aggrieved parties to step forward, under oath and in the glare of a high-profile trial, and testify. Shortly after the Appeals Court decision came down, Reback had breakfast with Klein in Washington and found the assistant attorney general in a nerve-addled state. "We've filed this thing," Klein said, "but we have no witnesses."

"If I were Joel, I would have been pissing my pants right then," Reback recalled. "The judge said 12 witnesses. I kept looking at my fingers and thinking, how are we ever going to get there?"

The only way, in Reback's view, was for the DOJ to somehow cut through the toxic mixture of fear of Microsoft and cynicism about the government's competence—the latter being at least as poisonous as the former—that hung like smog over Silicon Valley. In the tech world, the memory of the 1995 consent decree, seen universally as a dismal failure, remained fresh. And even with the Sherman Act case, the current crop of trustbusters hadn't gone very far toward instilling confidence in the DOJ. "There was a lot of trepidation in the Valley about whether the government was capable of getting any of this right," Reback remembered. "Nobody wanted to get anywhere near this thing. Nobody wanted to be subpoenaed. Nobody was sure they could pull it off."

Such was the climate of uncertainty and doubt when the hunt for witnesses began. Reback, naturally, joined in to help the DOJ; so did Orrin Hatch and Mike Hirshland. Playing every angle, pulling every string, Klein's team of 20-odd lawyers talked with dozens of the companies in Microsoft's crosshairs. Software companies and hardware companies. Internet infants and Fortune 500 stalwarts. They talked with Yahoo!, Excite, RealNetworks, Palm. And with most of the OEMs—Compaq, Acer, Gateway, Packard Bell, HP, Sony. Yet by the middle of July, the DOJ's witness list was so barren that Klein was considering filling a quarter of his slots with Netscape executives, another slot with someone from Sun, and many of the rest with economists and technical experts. He didn't have much choice. After several weeks of tree-shaking, the DOJ's efforts had produced a meager harvest.

And then, quite suddenly, some fruit began to fall.

■ ■ ■

IT BEGAN with Intuit, whose CEO, Bill Campbell, was a former college football coach who had received his share of bruises from butting heads with Gates. In the early 1980s, Campbell worked at Apple and helped launch the Macintosh, which depended on Microsoft applications to find its place in the market. Later in the decade, he became CEO of the doomstruck pen-computing company GO, whose flagship product was a bulkier, clumsier, costlier precursor to the Palm Pilot. For years after GO went belly-up, its executives blamed Gates, accusing him of stealing their ideas in order to build a copycat product and of pressuring OEMs not to ally with the start-up. In particular, they believed Microsoft had nixed a deal with Compaq that might have pulled GO back from the brink of bankruptcy. "We heard Gates came in personally and made Eckhard Pfeiffer [Compaq's then-CEO] an offer he couldn't refuse on the operating system—a big price cut on Windows—if Eckhard would forget about our deal and go with Microsoft's product instead," Campbell recalled. "We heard it from good sources, but we could never prove it."

At Intuit, Campbell and board member John Doerr (who bankrolled Intuit and GO) were, in Campbell's words, "the last holdouts" when the firm's chairman, Scott Cook, wanted to sell the company to Microsoft back in 1995. After the DOJ scotched the deal, Microsoft waged a fierce campaign to topple Intuit in the financial-software market. Against the odds, Campbell prevailed, doing whatever was necessary—including abandoning an alliance with Netscape—to maintain Intuit's place on the Windows desktop.

The DOJ had long suspected Intuit had a story to tell. In its court papers, the government cited a Microsoft email in which Gates wrote, "I was quite frank with [Cook] that if he had a favor we could do for him that would cost us something like $1M . . . in return for switching browsers in the next few months I would be open to doing that." But Campbell wanted no part of the DOJ. He regarded its lawyers as woefully overmatched ("I told them, the Bill Neukoms of the world are going to cream you government pantywaists") and the suit's short-term remedy as worse than meaningless ("They've got to put both browsers in the OS? Great. Now I have to pay double ransom"). Then that summer Campbell got a call from Hirshland, who told him the DOJ had hard evidence that Microsoft had indeed killed the Compaq deal which might have saved GO. Campbell also received a call from Hirshland's boss. "You know damn well there is some unethical behavior out there that's possibly illegal," Hatch said. "The only way we can expand the case is if people like you are willing to talk."

By late July, Campbell was seriously wavering, and he wanted to hear the opinions of Intuit's board and senior staff. At a three-hour meeting the debate was engaged. Speaking in favor of putting someone forward to testify was Doerr, who argued, "If we feel we're getting screwed, we ought to say so." Against the idea was Cook, who said helping the government would be an admission of defeat and a sign of weakness; it would put Intuit on a par with Silicon Valley's congenital complainers. Finally, a vote was taken: all except Cook agreed that Intuit should testify. For Campbell, it basically came down to a matter of cojones. "I thought, goddammit, forget the marketplace reaction, forget Microsoft's reaction. We ought to be strong enough to stand up and be counted."

Just around the time that Campbell was climbing on board, the DOJ caught another big break. The government investigators had been trying for months, without much luck, to nail down rumors that several years earlier Microsoft had strong-armed its ally Intel over Intel's plans regarding the Internet. Now, as the DOJ was taking depositions from various Netscape officials, Jim Clark recalled that an Intel executive named Steve McGeady had once told him about a meeting in which Gates had declared his intent to "take Netscape's air." Clark shot off an email to McGeady asking if he'd be willing to talk to the DOJ. McGeady wrote back almost instantly, correcting Clark's memory (it was Maritz, not Gates, who'd alluded to Netscape's impending lack of oxygen) but adding, "If the DOJ asks me to testify to that effect, I will, without hesitation." In short order, the government arranged to depose McGeady.

The DOJ should already have been aware of Steve McGeady. Three years earlier, on a tip from Reback, the antitrust division had sent McGeady a CID for documents concerning a clash between Intel and Microsoft over an Intel software technology called Native Signal Processing (NSP). But like the ark of the covenant at the end of the first Indiana Jones movie, the NSP documents had apparently been buried deep in the bowels of the DOJ, and the entire issue had faded from the department's collective memory—and from Intel's too. "Four days before my deposition, I say to my Intel lawyer, I assume you've reviewed the documents from 1995," McGeady recalled. "He says, 'What documents?' He doesn't know. So he calls the Justice Department. They don't know either!" McGeady rolled his eyes. "It was like the Keystone Kops do antitrust."

McGeady's deposition was dynamite stuff. Yet the DOJ's dealings with Intel were wary and delicate. For nearly 20 years, Intel and Microsoft had collaborated so closely that they were often regarded as a unitary being: "Wintel." The moniker was mislead-ing, for the relationship was riven with fractures and fissures. Andy Grove liked to refer to the companies not as strategic partners ("I really hate that phrase," he snarled) but as "fellow travelers"—not soulmates, but seatmates on the same train, whose journey together will eventually end. Yet because Intel was hugely dependent on Microsoft, and vice versa, keeping peace with Gates was one of Grove's prime priorities. So when Intel finally acknowledged that McGeady would be testifying in the trial, the company took pains to assume a posture of perfect neutrality. McGeady was not being "sent" to testify; he was merely being "allowed" to testify. What choice do we have? Intel asked, in effect. The government wants him; we can hardly refuse.

Behind the scenes, though, Intel's neutrality was far from perfect. With the stealth and finesse of an accomplished Byzantine courtier, the company's general counsel, Peter Detkin, was helping drive the stiletto into Microsoft's back. Detkin was a former partner at Wilson Sonsini, where he had worked with Reback on a number of cases. There was no love lost between the two, but over the years Reback had conducted what he called "deep-throat meetings" with Detkin and other Intel lawyers in the bar at Hyatt Rickeys in Palo Alto. When the government started asking questions about McGeady, Detkin turned to Reback and Susan Creighton as a covert back-channel to the DOJ. "Peter used Wilson Sonsini as a safe conduit to pass information to the government," a lawyer close to the situation said. "The nature of the information was: If you look here, or here, or here, you'll find something interesting." Indeed, in the final analysis, Detkin seemed to have been the source, in this roundabout way, of most of the Intel leads that would bear fruit for the DOJ.

When a story that the DOJ had deposed various Intel executives splashed across the front page of *The New York Times* in late

August, the news hit Silicon Valley like a thunderbolt from a clear blue sky. If Intel was cooperating with the government (as everyone assumed it was, no matter what the company was saying publicly), then the DOJ's case was undeniably gathering steam. "Part of the calculus on every witness's part was, Who else is testifying?" Boies recalled. "Once you get a couple of witnesses in the box, you can tell other people you've got them, and your life becomes much easier." With Intel and Intuit in the box, Boies was able to lock down witnesses from two companies with which he had tight connections: IBM, where the ancient Microsoft hatreds still burned, and AOL, whose head of government affairs, George Vradenburg, had previously been in-house counsel to CBS and had hired Boies to handle the Westmoreland libel case.

The DOJ got another boost with Judge Jackson's decision in mid-September to delay the trial's start until mid-October. The extra month would buy the DOJ some breathing room. It would also provide a chance to go after the most glittering prize of all: Steve Jobs and Apple.

THE DOJ'S interest in Apple was twofold. The first element was the headline-grabbing deal between Cupertino and Redmond in August 1997, in which, the government believed, Microsoft had threatened to cancel Office for the Macintosh unless Apple replaced Navigator with IE as the Mac's default browser. The second was multimedia. The DOJ had recently received from Reback another of his inimitable white papers, this one focused on the Apple multimedia technology QuickTime. The Apple white paper alleged that over the previous two years Microsoft had engaged in a passel of predatory tactics to stifle QuickTime—tactics that loudly echoed its approach to Netscape's browser. According to the Reback brief, Microsoft had proposed carving up the multimedia market with Apple; it had then pressured OEMs to drop Quick-Time; it had inserted technical incompatibilities that disabled QuickTime in Windows; and it had struck exclusionary deals with content providers to develop only for Microsoft's competing Net-Show technology. At one point, a Microsoft business-development manager had made a suggestion about what Apple should do to its own newborn technology, which was so irresistibly colorful that Reback made it the white paper's title: "Knife the Baby."

In the autumn of 1998, Apple's recovery under Jobs was still tenuous and fragile, and the company's relationship with Microsoft remained as precarious as ever. If the DOJ had a prayer of inducing Apple to throw caution aside and sign up for the trial, Reback was the man to see. In the fevered quest for fresh evidence and plausible witnesses, whatever lingering resentments Klein harbored toward the monomaniacal lawyer had receded. Reback was simply too useful, too plugged-in and switched-on, to be ignored. In a series of phone calls that September, Klein told Reback he desperately wanted the Apple story to be part of the trial—and he wanted Jobs to be the one to tell it. Though the DOJ's witness list was shaping up nicely, Klein was concerned that it lacked star power, featuring as it did only one marquee-quality CEO: Jim Barksdale. Klein told Reback, "We have an *übermenschen* problem."

Jobs was certainly *über*, but no one had ever accused him of being a mensch. Visionary, volatile, volcanic, and vain, Apple's founder minced no words regarding his skepticism about the DOJ's capacity to prosecute Microsoft. "The government is bullshit! The government is bullshit!" he had barked when a government lawyer visited him that spring to ask for his help in building the case. For the next twenty minutes, Jobs uncorked a vintage screed against Gates's company, about how its monopoly was "chilling innovation" and "fundamentally poisoning" the software industry. Then he shifted his scorn back to the government. "You guys have done nothing, you haven't figured it out, you've been too slow, you'll never change anything. This is an incredibly sensitive time for Apple. Why should I jeopardize the future of my company when I have no faith that the government is going to do anything real?"

To Jobs, "real" meant one thing: breaking Microsoft up. For all his doubts about the DOJ's competence, he was now grudgingly impressed by the government's progress. In late September, after several lengthy talks with Reback, his friend Bill Campbell, and a number of DOJ intermediaries in the Valley, Jobs agreed to have a conversation with Klein about the possibility of testifying. When the two men connected by phone, with Jobs on vacation in Hawaii, he wasted no time in getting to the point. He wanted to hear Klein's thoughts on remedies.

"Are you going to do something serious?" Jobs demanded. "Or is it going to be dickless?"

At the other end of the line, Klein squirmed. Even if he had settled on a remedy, which he hadn't, it would have been grossly inappropriate to discuss it with Jobs—or with any other Microsoft competitor. Klein told Jobs this. He told him he could offer him no commitments, no promises. Klein said, "It's a chicken-and-egg problem; the power of the remedy will be determined by the quality of the case."

Jobs was singularly unimpressed, and he let Reback know it. Frustrated, Reback called Mike Hirshland to commiserate. "Joel blew it," Reback sighed. Jobs hadn't needed a firm commitment. What he needed was to be sold on the notion that the DOJ was, à la Microsoft, hard-core about the case. But Klein hadn't been selling; he'd been legalistic, stilted, excessively circumspect. He'd been . . . Joel.

As Hirshland listened to Reback moan, he had a brainstorm. Why not have Boies give Jobs a call? Not being a DOJ official, the litigator might have more freedom to deliver a proper pitch. After hanging up with Reback, Hirshland called Boies and ran the idea past him. Sure, Boies said, but he would need Klein's blessing. "It might be delicate," Boies went on. "Can you get Senator Hatch to call Joel and tell him this needs to happen?"

Meanwhile, Reback had had a bright idea of his own. Realizing that part of Jobs's reluctance to testify revolved around the fear (a rare one for him) of standing alone at center stage, of being by far the most significant person in computing to be opposing Gates in so public a forum, Reback suggested to Apple's CEO that perhaps there was a way to give him some cover. What if another industry figure of Jobs's stature were to testify alongside him? Jobs liked the idea, but to his mind there was only one person who belonged in that category: Andy Grove.

Thus began a brief but frantic spell during which the DOJ and much of the anti-Microsoft movement was seized by the most hallucinatory of fantasies: the Grove-Jobs twofer—get one, get both.

And a fantasy is precisely what it was. Not only was Grove the archetypal practitioner of corporate realpolitik, but at that moment Intel was engulfed in a substantial antitrust inquiry of its own, conducted by the FTC. In any sane universe, the proposition that Grove might be cajoled into taking the stand against Gates would have seemed only marginally more tenable than the proposition that Steve Ballmer might join him in the witness box.

Yet with less than three weeks to go before the trial, the prevailing atmosphere at the DOJ was not exactly one of cold-eyed

Court of Appeals
chief justice Richard
Posner.

(Reuters New Media Inc./Corbis)

U.S. district judge Thomas Penfield Jackson. *(Reuters/Larry Downing/Archive Photos)*

Bill Gates at a Council on Foreign Relations reception in his honor.

(David Burnett/Contact Press Images)

rationality. Thus, during the last week of September, did Andy Grove discover how it feels to be the most sought-after man in Silicon Valley. At Yom Kippur services, Reback sat down beside Intel's Peter Detkin and whispered, "We have to talk." Soon Detkin found himself on the phone with Klein. At home, Grove was deluged with plaintive calls from the DOJ's surrogates. He heard from various Valley figures, from Hatch, and even from Jobs. What none of these suitors knew was that Grove was at the same time fielding entreaties from Gates and Neukom, who were begging him to testify on Microsoft's behalf. Grove's reply to both sides was the same: Intel is neutral in this case and so am I. Besides, he said, any testimony he offered would be a double-edged sword. "I've been in the middle of all this shit for years," Grove told me. "I don't lie. I particularly don't lie under oath. And I really particularly don't lie under oath when there is no reason to. I would have said things that neither side would have been happy to hear."

With Grove's irrevocable refusal, the DOJ lost its chance at Jobs. By the time Boies called Apple's CEO, "He'd made up his mind," the lawyer recalled. "He just didn't want to testify." Yet in failing to land Silicon Valley's two reigning kingfish, the DOJ came away with two less spectacular but important victories. All along in its dealings with Intel, the government had feared being double-crossed; that, under pressure from Gates, the company would provide a witness, perhaps even Grove, for the defense. But now Grove had given his word that this wouldn't happen. And while Jobs would not testify himself, he pledged to send Avie Tevanian in his stead. In Boies's view, this was no small thing. "While not having the star power of Jobs, Tevanian had a fair amount of star power of his own, just a different kind. And he could speak to some of these issues in a way that was even stronger than Jobs could have," Boies said. "Now, that was not a universally held opinion in the Justice Department, but I felt quite satisfied."

By early October, with the inclusion of Tevanian and another software expert, James Gosling of Sun, the DOJ's witness list was complete. In the end, it had only one gaping hole: the absence of an OEM official to testify about the ways Microsoft leveraged its Windows monopoly to exert coercive power over computer manufacturers. (The witness from IBM, John Soyring, would talk only about the development of OS/2.) The search for an OEM whistleblower had consumed more man-hours at the DOJ than securing any other witness, but no amount of suasion was enough to convince PC makers that they had more to gain than lose by airing their grievances. "Most of the major OEMs are simply afraid," Klein said at the time. "A lot of them said to us, 'What you're doing is terrific, but we just can't afford to stick out our necks.' The power that Microsoft has over these people with the Windows license and the Office license is simply extraordinary."

The failure to land an OEM was frustrating for Klein, but it did nothing to diminish his sense of how far his team had come. Three months earlier, the government had been staring at the prospect of going up against Microsoft wielding nothing but Netscape and a handful of academics. Now it was armed with a roster of the industry's heaviest heavyweights: Intel, IBM, Apple, AOL, Sun, and Intuit. Boies's warning to Gates and Neukom back in May had proven eerily prophetic: the lawsuit really had changed everything, emboldening Microsoft's enemies and turning one of its most steadfast allies against it.

After months of anxiety and hand-wringing, Boies and Klein were happy warriors—happier, actually, than anyone realized. For the DOJ's lawyers knew something few others did: they had a surprise witness up their sleeves. A witness of unimpeachable authority. A witness with power beyond reckoning and cash beyond counting. A witness guaranteed to overshadow even the brightest lights on the list they'd announced. A witness—need it be said?—who would soon have Microsoft's defenders paraphrasing Pogo: We have seen the enemy, and he is Gates.

IF THE government's trial preparations had the flavor of a blitzkrieg, Microsoft's were carried out with the methodical discipline of a Prussian counteroffensive—and predictably so, given the fellow commanding the company's legal battalions. Stylistically, Bill Neukom was an odd man out at Microsoft. He was in his fifties, with a wavy pompadour of silver hair, a handsome face, and a patrician air. He was tall and trim and impeccably dressed, his suits well-pressed and accented with braces and florid bow ties. Polite and formal, Neukom spoke in precise sentences that he strung together to form perfect paragraphs. He was occasionally turgid and always verbose. Once, after I'd finished a long interview with him, another Microsoft executive remarked, "I'm sure he crammed 20 minutes of substance into those two hours."

Neukom had grown up in northern California, where his father cofounded and oversaw the San Francisco office of McKinsey & Company. After graduating from Dartmouth and Stanford Law, he moved to Seattle in 1967, where he eventually landed at the law firm of Bill Gates's father. The elder Gates handpicked Neukom to handle his son's legal affairs, on the basis, Bill Sr. has said, that Neukom was "mentally agile" and "didn't have an exceptional level of ego." Before going to work in-house at Microsoft, Neukom, a liberal Democrat, had a brief flirtation with politics. In 1980, he sought his party's nomination as Washington State's attorney general but finished second. Thereafter, his interest in public affairs was channeled into philanthropy; the Neukom Family Foundation has steered millions of dollars into education and health-care programs.

Neukom became Microsoft's general counsel in 1985. Three years later, the company was hit with the Apple copyright suit, which threatened, Gates said, to "absolutely put us out of business." The case dragged on for five years, and the received wisdom in the press was that Microsoft was in the wrong, that it had plainly ripped off Apple's graphical user interface to create Windows. But Neukom advised Gates to ignore the punditry and focus on the law, which the attorney was certain supported Microsoft's position. The court's vindication of that view, in 1993, was Neukom's greatest triumph, and a source of Gates's trust in his judgment.

In combating the government, Neukom presided over a squadron of lawyers three times the size of the DOJ's. Although attorneys from Sullivan & Cromwell would handle a fair amount of the heavy lifting, and especially the courtroom work, there was no question as to which of the lawyers was in charge. "Neukom is the guy who conducts the orchestra," Klein said. "He doesn't move the stick, but you can almost feel the energy shift when he's ready to have X stop talking and Y start talking."

Just as he had in the Apple dispute, Neukom believed unequivocally that the law was on Microsoft's side. To prove it, he and his team set out over the summer of 1998 to pull together evidence to show that, far from being a monopolist, Microsoft faced competition from all sides; that the company's contracts with OEMs and ISPs were commonplace in the industry; that the infamous June 1995 meeting with Netscape was nothing more than a routine powwow between an operating-system vendor and an applications provider; that integrating IE into Windows wasn't part of a nefarious plot to wipe out Netscape but rather a natural extension of the OS, just as Microsoft's past inclusion of features such as printer drivers and memory management had been; that, in fact, the company's plans to incorporate browsing into Windows had begun before Netscape had even been born. In support of these claims, the team came up with hundreds of internal documents and email. They took dozens of depositions. And they assembled a witness list composed almost entirely of Microsoft executives, who would tell the company's story in court.

As the Microsoft lawyers readied their case, the most potent of all their potential witnesses dropped out of sight. In late July, Gates named Steve Ballmer Microsoft's president, as his board of directors had been urging him to do for months. In an email to employees, Gates wrote that, from then on, Ballmer and Bob Herbold would be responsible for running the company day-to-day, while he would spend his time on product development and new technology. "In no way am I pulling back," Gates wrote. "The hours I put in and my enjoyment of the work I do will be absolutely the same." And with that, he took off on a weeks-long vacation.

In every respect, it was a billionaire's holiday. Accompanied by his wife, fellow plutocrats such as Warren Buffet and Will Hearst, Microsoft executives such as Jeff Raikes, and other chums, Gates chartered a train to ferry them around the American West on a sightseeing tour of its natural wonders. Fine food was consumed, slavish service provided. "Traveling with Bill is definitely a trip," one guest said. "There are all these minions, these courtiers, who make sure he never gets bored or testy. Then there are these experts who just appear out of nowhere. It's like, 'Who's the best archaeologist to explain this canyon? Bring him to me!' And the guy just magically appears!"

Yet even when Gates was at play, business and the trial were never far from his mind. In the presence of his traveling companions, Gates mused that Ballmer's elevation signaled the beginning of an orderly succession; within two or three years, Gates said, he might be ready to step down as CEO. And while Microsoft's flacks had been whispering all summer long to reporters that Gates wasn't intimately involved in preparing the company's legal defense, some of his guests came away with the opposite impression. "He seemed totally in the loop," a member of the group said. "He was aware of the issues, he'd read all the evidence and read up on the law, the procedures, the timing—everything." In fact, Gates told at least one person on the train trip that, although no final decision had been made, he expected to appear in court as one of Microsoft's witnesses.

Whether or not Gates took the stand, he knew the government intended to depose him. In Washington, a row had broken out over the conditions under which his questioning would occur. On one front, Microsoft's lawyers were seeking to limit the deposition to a single eight-hour day. On another, a clutch of media organizations, drawn like moths to the flames that a Gates-Boies face-off would inevitably spark, were demanding the right to attend the interrogation, citing an obscure 1913 statute which seemed to grant the public full access to any depositions in an antitrust case. After a flurry of briefs and an intercession by the Appeals Court, the government was ordered to conduct the Gates deposition (and all others) in private. But on the question of its duration, Judge Jackson had the final word: Boies could take as long as he needed.

Ten days before Gates was scheduled to be deposed by the DOJ, he jetted down to Silicon Valley for a dinner hosted by his friend Heidi Roizen. An entrepreneur and a former Apple executive, Roizen had recently signed on as Microsoft's informal ambassador to the Valley, her assignment being to improve the company's standing on hostile turf. "I joked with Bill, 'You know, you're going to hire me and the brilliant advice I'm going to have is that you should go to more parties down here, and you're going to cringe,' " Roizen said. To ease Gates's entrée, she had decided to throw him a party herself, inviting a handful of nonantagonistic Valley types such as Marimba CEO Kim Polese, the veteran software executive Gordon Eubanks, a young venture capitalist named Ted Schlein, and Gates's old flame Ann Winblad.

By all accounts, it was a bizarre soiree. Roizen and her husband, whose home in the ritzy Silicon Valley enclave of Atherton is a 7,000-square-foot spread with trompe l'oeil bookcases, buffalo heads on the walls, and a suit of medieval armor in the stairwell, had arranged for a "rooftop-golf" tournament in which their guests hit balls from atop the house at makeshift pins set up around the backyard. (The hot tub had been lined with Astro Turf for the occasion.) At dinner, Gates "geeked out," one participant said, regaling the table with tales of programs he'd written in Microsoft's early days and speaking admiringly about a book that he'd been reading: *Titan*, Ron Chernow's biography of J. D. Rockefeller. Later, the group made an excursion into Roizen's torchlit wine cellar and played high-tech trivia games until after midnight. (At trivia, unlike at golf, Gates won.)

The most surreal moment of all, however, took place early in the evening. The date of Roizen's dinner party was August 17, which history will record was the day Bill Clinton came clean with Ken Starr—and with the nation—admitting for the first time his dalliance with Monica Lewinsky. When Roizen's guests arrived at cocktail hour, they eagerly scurried upstairs to watch Clinton's prime-time speech on the big screen in their hosts' bedroom. Perched at the edge of the bed, Gates heckled the president mercilessly, with a degree of venom that took some of the others aback. Clinton was a loser, Gates said; his speech was "hot air," a "pile of crap." To more than one person, it seemed obvious that Gates blamed Clinton for his antitrust woes. "If I did what he did in my office," Gates squawked, "the shareholders would throw me out!"

On August 27, in a windowless conference room in Microsoft's Building 8, Gates sat down across from his own Ken Starr for an extended spell of exquisite torture. David Boies had prepared for the event in his own distinctive style. While Gates was swanning around the West via luxe rail, the lawyer was covering much the same ground in an open-topped Jeep on a road-trip vacation with one of his sons. The night before the deposition, Boies blew off an 80-page outline prepared by an associate and watched the movie *Tombstone* on television instead. Not that Boies was blasé about the task before him. "I expected the Bill Gates I'd be facing would be the same Bill Gates I'd been in a room with that spring," he said. "The Bill Gates I'd met was smart, tough, and articulate, a very passionate and effective spokesman for his point of view." Boies grinned. "Needless to say, that was not the Bill Gates who showed up for the deposition."

The Gates who showed up for the videotaped deposition was not only the polar opposite of his public persona, he was a carica-ture of the polar opposite. He was dour and cantankerous. He was petulant and passive-aggressive, obfuscatory and obscurantist. He was a quibbler, a pedant, an amnesiac, a baby. He was the sort of CEO who would profess not to recall countless emails he'd written and who would claim to be ignorant of his company's strategies—strategies he himself had masterminded. Who would quarrel stub-bornly over the meanings of words like "concern," "compete," "definition," "ask," and "very." Who would take five minutes to concede that when another Microsoft executive talked about "piss-ing on" Java, it was not, as Boies put it, a "code word that means saying nice things." Who, when asked who had attended a Microsoft executive-staff meeting, would reply, "Probably members of the executive staff."

For his part, Boies stayed cool. He was patient and persistent, asking certain questions again and again and again, often using precisely the same phrasing, until Gates either coughed up a straight answer or provided Boies an equally valuable display of prevarication. Early on, the lawyer remarked placidly, "I've got as much time as I need to finish the examination, sir, and I'm prepared to spend as many days here as I have to." In the end, that would be three, yielding 20 hours of Bill Gates unplugged.

At the end of the first day, Boies phoned Klein. "They're never going to call him as a witness now," he said confidently.

Klein was incredulous. "Well, that's not what we've heard," he replied. "We've heard they're telling everybody they're going to bring him."

"They're not going to bring him. He's already said too many things he could never explain on the stand."

At the end of the second day, although Boies hadn't yet covered all the ground he intended to, he was so delighted with the material he'd already garnered that he seriously considered ending the deposition right there. Gates was headed off for a long weekend on an Alaskan cruise hosted by Paul Allen, and Boies, already perplexed that Gates's lawyers hadn't stepped in to curb his behavior, assumed his quarry would return in greater command of himself. But Boies decided to risk it. On the third day, his reward—among others—was one of the deposition's genuinely priceless exchanges. Handing Gates an email he'd written, Boies offhandedly remarked that at the top of the message Gates had typed "Importance: High."

"No," Gates said curtly.

"No?"

"No, I didn't type that."

Then who did?

"A computer."

"A computer. Why did the computer type in 'High'?"

"It's an attribute of the email."

"And who sets the attribute of the email?"

"Usually the sender sets that attribute."

"Who is the sender here, Mr. Gates?"

"In this case, it appears I'm the sender."

"Yes. And so you're the one who set the high designation of importance, right, sir?"

"It appears I did that."

Gates's performance was an unmitigated disaster, and not only in terms of PR. As a piece of evidence, it handed Boies the largest, most gnarled club imaginable with which to bludgeon both Gates and Microsoft as a whole, for the deposition fairly screamed that the dissembling at the company started at the top. It was a point that would not be lost on Judge Jackson. "Here is the guy who is the head of the organization, and his testimony is inherently without credibility," he said in an interview that appeared after the case was over. "At the start, it makes you skeptical about the rest of the trial. You are saying, if you can't believe this guy, who else can you believe?"

Many observers would blame Gates's lawyers for the deposition fiasco, but Boies believed it wasn't that simple. "I've said many times that if I had been his attorney I would have stopped the deposition," Boies said. "But the thing I don't know, and the thing nobody will know unless I get Bill Neukom more drunk than he should be, is how much of it was the lawyers' unwillingness to act and how much of it was the client rejecting their absolutely unambiguous instructions." Not surprisingly, Boies had his suspicions. "You have in Gates someone who is very smart, very rich, very powerful, and very much in command. He's a very hard client to say no to."

Very hard—perhaps impossible. Since Microsoft's birth, Gates had seen himself as its chief legal strategist, Bill Neukom's presence notwithstanding. Reared in a lawyerly household, schooled by his father in lawyerly thinking, Gates's lawyerly proclivities shaped the company and the software business profoundly. It was Gates who, in 1976, published a kind of manifesto, "An Open Letter to Hobbyists," in an early computer newsletter, which asserted for the first time that software, like hardware, was a valuable commodity—it was intellectual property, and as such its creators deserved to be compensated. It was Gates whose grasp of the fine points of contracts had allowed him to outmaneuver IBM in the MS-DOS deal that would be the foundation of Microsoft's empire. And for all the accolades heaped on Neukom for the outcome of the Apple suit, the greater credit actually belonged to his boss. "Neukom did yeoman's work, but make no mistake, it was Bill who won the Apple case," a former Microsoft executive asserted. "He was deeply engaged in the case, he knew the issues, both technical and legal, and he played a huge role in framing them for the court. Hell, he practically wrote our briefs himself."

Among Microsoft executives a commonly repeated conceit was that Gates was not only smarter than his lawyers but had a greater mastery of the law than they did. It was a conceit Gates himself seemed to believe. As the Sherman Act trial drew near, he boned up on antitrust, studying the case law, poring over precedents. "Bill knows the courts to an amazing degree," a senior Microsoft manager said. "He knows all about the judges—who they are, how they've decided in the past, district by district, all over the country. This is not a normal client who just sits across from his lawyers and takes their advice. No way."

Even after the trial was long past, Gates continued to insist, and not unemotionally, that his deposition performance was badly and even maliciously mischaracterized. He answered honestly and precisely, he said. He seemed especially wounded by those who used the video to portray him as forgetful. Again and again, in *Rain Man*–like cadences, he declared, "I have an excellent memory, a most excellent memory." He asked rhetorically, "Did I fence with Boies? I plead guilty. Whatever that penalty is should be levied against me: rudeness to Boies in the first degree." He allowed that his tone of voice was regrettable, as were the camera angles. Yet, at bottom, all this was mere atmospherics, he said, and therefore irrelevant.

Microsoft's lawyers were a mite less sanguine. Compelled by reality (and a concern for their own reputations) to acknowledge the damage done by the Gates tapes, they blamed Judge Jackson, who had issued a pretrial order that led them to believe the tapes would not be shown in court. Had they thought otherwise, Neukom maintained, they would have prepared Gates differently—if only in terms of style. (They would also have made sure the lighting was more flattering.)

Boies scoffed at Microsoft's contention that the company didn't realize the tapes would be aired: "What, they thought I was taking them for my memory book?" He offered his own theory, which revolved around Gates's assumption going into the deposition that he would be called as a witness by one side or the other. "He must have thought that if he came as a witness, we wouldn't be able to introduce the videotape," Boies said. "And he was probably right about that. If he had been a witness, I don't think the judge would have let us play it. As a result, he wasn't really focused on how he looked in the deposition. He was prepared to stonewall. He was prepared to do all kinds of things that you might do if you believed nobody was going to see it."

Instead, the degree of Gates's stonewalling was so great, and his evasions were so egregious, that the deposition set in motion a cascade of unintended consequences. Suddenly, Microsoft had little alternative but to keep its most powerful witness off the stand, lest he be humiliated in the futile attempt to defend the indefensible and explain the inexplicable. The DOJ, meanwhile, now had no reason to call Gates, for whatever he said in the courtroom could hardly serve the government's purposes more effectively than the testimony it already had in the can. The world's richest man had no date to the dance. And the video was fair game.

"It was like the Russian Revolution," Boies concluded. "Everything had to fall into place just so for it to turn out as it did."

LIKE THE czars in Petrograd in 1917, Microsoft in the late summer of 1998 could feel the ground shifting beneath its feet. Nearly a year had passed since the DOJ filed the consent-decree case, and in that time, almost everything that could possibly go wrong had. Surrounded by Bolsheviks and Mensheviks, populists and nihilists, the old regime began, for the first time, to betray a hint of what Gates, on a carefree day, would have called "concern," but that others might properly have described as panic. With the government's new evidence and witnesses from Apple, Intel, Intuit, and the rest, what had once looked to Microsoft like a simple tying case was taking on the countenance of something far bigger—and far uglier. "They converted a Sherman Act case into a business tort trial," Neukom said later. "It was clear they were going to sell the judge and the public an image of a company that couldn't be trusted and ought to be penalized."

Trying to roll back the tide, Microsoft flooded Judge Jackson's chambers with pretrial motions—nine of them in September and October. The motions' themes cried out from their titles: "Motion to Limit Issues for Trial"; "Arguments for Excluding Extraneous Last-Minute Issues from Trial"; "Motion for a Continuance Needed to Address Testimony of Plaintiffs' New Trial Witnesses"; and so on. The case the government had filed in May, Microsoft argued, was all about browsers and a tad about Java. Broadening it beyond those issues was illegitimate, unfair, and a sign that the DOJ realized the Appeals Court's decision had "eviscerated" the core of its original complaint. At the very least, Microsoft said, the company needed more time to build a thorough defense.

The DOJ's response was swift, emphatic, and gently mocking. In one of its reply briefs, the government wrote: "To the limited extent that plaintiffs offer evidence adduced in discovery concerning events and transactions not strictly limited to browsers and Java, those events and transactions (a) directly evidence monopoly power and barriers to entry, which issues are (of course) part of plaintiffs' complaints, and of every Sherman Act Section 2 case; (b) demonstrate Microsoft's intent to monopolize, which issue is (of course) also part of plaintiffs' complaints, and of every Sherman Act Section 2 attempt case: and/or (c) demonstrate a pattern that is relevant to understanding and establishing Microsoft's conduct with respect to browsers and Java." The DOJ's Jeff Blattner put it more colorfully: "We haven't broadened the case—we've broadened the evidence. In a murder case, you refer to the body in the filing. But at trial you bring out the bloody glove, the bloody shoes, the murder weapon."

Right up to the eve of the trial, the back-and-forth between the sides continued unabated. But with every volley, the referee remained consistent. Time and again, in written orders and pre-trial hearings, Judge Jackson informed Microsoft that the trial would be broad, and that it would focus on one large question: whether the company had "maintained its operating-system monopoly through exclusionary and predatory conduct." As Jackson put it matter-of-factly to Neukom and his team, "My view of the case is not as narrow as yours."

And so it was that, on the morning of October 19, the courtroom phase of the Microsoft case began. For three solid hours, David Boies, slightly stoned on antihistamines and armed with only a few scribbled notes on one side of a manila folder, held the room pretty much in the palm of his hand. There was nothing soaring about his oratory, nothing ornate or mellifluous. Instead, the power of his opening lay in the narrative he unfurled and the evidence he unveiled in support of it. The story he told was straightforward: faced with the threat posed by the browser and Java, Microsoft had tried first to coerce Netscape into not competing with it; after being rebuffed, it had put the screws to the entire industry in an effort to destroy the start-up and keep its grip on the desktop. As he walked Judge Jackson through the government's claims, Boies displayed on the courtroom monitors a sequence of documents that painted Gates and Microsoft as the most rapacious (and unsubtle) of monopolists. There was an AOL email describing an offer from Microsoft's CEO: "Gates delivered a characteristically blunt query: how much do we need to pay you to screw Netscape? ('This is your lucky day')." There was a memo from a Hewlett-Packard manager complaining about Microsoft's refusal to allow HP to change the first screen on its machines: "If we had a choice of another supplier, based on your actions, I assure you that you would not be our supplier of choice." And, the pièce de résistance, there was Gates unplugged.

On four different occasions, electrifying the courtroom, Boies played video excerpts from the deposition, each time juxtaposing them with contemporaneous documents that revealed Gates, to put it gently, as less than totally candid. Here was Microsoft's CEO on screen, denying knowledge of the June 1995 meeting—saying, indeed, "I had no sense of what Netscape was doing" at the time. And here was an email from Gates to Maritz and other Microsoft brass a few weeks before the meeting: "I think there is a very powerful deal of some kind we can do with Netscape. . . . We could even pay them money as part of the deal, buying some piece of them or something. I would really like to see something like this happen!!"

When Boies was done and the court gaveled out of session, Neukom appeared before a gaggle of reporters on the courthouse steps. Calmly but adamantly, he denounced Boies's tactics as hollow theatrics, accusing him of using "loose rhetoric and out-of-context snippets" to disguise the fact that he had no case and adding that "none of these snippets, none of this rhetoric, even approaches proof of anticompetitive conduct."

The next day, Klein jetted down to Scottsdale, Arizona. On the one-year anniversary of the filing of the consent-decree case, he was scheduled to give a keynote address at Agenda, the conference at which Gates first heard the news that his government was suing him. The speech Klein would deliver was a high-minded affair, a discussion of regulation, market failure, and "the case for government involvement in the computer industry." He would offer few comments on the trial, and those he did offer were as dry and arid as the high-desert air. Klein knew better than anyone that the government had a long row to hoe. He expected Microsoft to mount an awesome defense. And he knew that one good day in court was no cause for chest-thumping.

Still, that one good day had been a very good day. In the back of the hall, Klein whispered to me, "I am one happy camper. We really kicked their butts."

Chapter Five

IN THE DOCK

THE E. BARRETT PRETTYMAN federal courthouse squatted at the northwest edge of Capitol Hill and bore all the hallmarks of the neo-brutalist architectural style that came into vogue in Washington in the 1950s. The six-story facade was gray and granite and imposingly free of inspiration. Inside, the walls were of marble— light gray streaked with darker gray. Down in the basement, a bare-bones cafeteria served food, also gray, to the several hundred maintenance people and clerks who worked in the building. (The judges tended to take their meals elsewhere—in Judge Jackson's case, at his club, the Metropolitan.) And yet, however mundane its appearance, the courthouse had provided the setting for more historic legal confrontations than any place save the Supreme Court itself. The Watergate trials, the arguments over the Pentagon Papers, the Whitewater/Lewinsky grand jury hearings—all were conducted here, at the corner of Constitution Avenue and Third Street, NW.

The Microsoft trial took place on the second floor, in Courtroom No. 2, a small space with five rows of hard wooden pews in the back providing seats for just 100 spectators. Given the level of interest among the press, Judge Jackson had been urged to hear the case in the large ceremonial courtroom upstairs. But Courtroom 2 was where Judge John J. Sirica had tried the Watergate defendants, and Jackson told his clerks, "This case ain't any bigger than that one." In addition to being relatively cramped, the courtroom was windowless, airless, and charmless, bathed in fluorescent light and perfumed with the scent of stale arguments and fresh acrimony. In the absence of a jury, the jury box was occupied by sketch artists, who often surveyed the scene through special eyewear that resembled the night-vision goggles worn by Navy SEALs and Green Berets.

The lawyers from each side huddled around tables at Jackson's feet. Based strictly on appearances, it wasn't hard to see why oddsmakers favored Microsoft's team, which was composed of men in slick suits with hard eyes and harder hair. The government's table, by contrast, had a slightly ragtag look to it, the clothes off-the-rack, the coiffures pure Supercuts. Even Boies, with his mail-order apparel and scuffed black sneakers, could easily have passed for a GS-11 from the Department of Agriculture.

As much as the government's case had widened, its sine qua non remained Netscape, so the first witness Boies called was Jim Barksdale. Dressed in a gray suit, a white shirt, and a red tie, with a pair of reading glasses perched at the end of his nose, Barksdale displayed no shortage of gravitas. His resume included stints as a salesman for IBM, chief operating officer of Federal Express, and president of McCaw Cellular Communications (and briefly president of AT&T Wireless Services, as McCaw was called after AT&T acquired it in 1994). At 55, he had a ruddy complexion that reddened appreciably when he was annoyed or incensed—which he would be quite a lot in the days ahead.

The job of questioning him fell to Microsoft's lead litigator, John Warden, a Sullivan & Cromwell partner with great experience in antitrust. In 1979, Warden had won the Appeals Court decision in *Berkey Photo v. Kodak*, a seminal ruling which held that "any firm, even a monopolist, may generally bring its products to market whenever and however it chooses. " A rotund man with dark-framed glasses, Warden, who had grown up in Evansville, Indiana, spoke in a deep Southern drawl that rose up from his thorax like a foghorn booming from the bottom of a well. (In private, Barksdale and Netscape's attorneys nicknamed him "Boomer.") Between the lawyer and the witness, a Mississippi native, there were times when, if you closed your eyes, you could imagine you were in a county courthouse far below the Mason-Dixon line. While Warden mangled the names of Netscape's multiethnic employees, Barksdale peppered his answers with downhomeisms such as "We put a little Kentucky windage on it" and "That irritated the stew out of me."

Barksdale's written testimony ran to 126 pages, and Warden appeared intent on refuting every one of its 251 paragraphs. No assertion was too trivial to contest, no detail too minute to challenge. Yet the matter that drew the most sustained fire was Barksdale's account of the June 1995 meeting. In his direct written testimony, Barksdale had stated, "I have never been in a [business] meeting in my 33-year business career in which a competitor had so blatantly implied that we should either stop competing with it or the competitor would kill us. In all my years in business, I have never heard nor experienced such an explicit proposal to divide markets."

Warden posited that, far from being a feared aggressor, Microsoft had been invited—no, begged—to do a deal by Netscape. In support of this assertion, the lawyer produced an email from Jim Clark to the senior Microsoft executive Brad Silverberg, sent at 3:01 A.M. on December 29, 1994. "We have never planned to compete with you," Clark had written. "We want to make this company a success, but not at Microsoft's expense. We'd like to work with you. Working together could be in your self-interest as well as ours. Depending on the interest level, you might take an equity position in Netscape, with the ability to expand the position later."

Barksdale reeled. At the time the email was sent, he had been a few days away from taking over as Netscape's CEO; he had had no idea what Clark was up to. In preparing for the trial, Barksdale had learned from Clark's deposition that there had been some late-night missive, but Clark hadn't mentioned, as Barksdale put it later, "that he was basically trying to sell the company." Now Barksdale told the court that Clark had written the email in a "moment of weakness." He said Clark had been freelancing, that his note never represented the company's official or unofficial strategy. But as Barksdale stared at the email on the courtroom monitor, all he could think to himself was, "Well, goddamn."

Warden asked Barksdale if Clark enjoyed "a public reputation for veracity."

Long pause. "I couldn't comment on that," Barksdale said. "I don't know."

"Do you regard him as a truthful man?"

Even longer pause. "I regard him as a salesman."

Throughout the Microsoft trial there would be moments that revealed what the journalist Joseph Nocera called "the secret history of the software industry." This was one of them. To a Silicon Valley outsider, Barksdale's disavowals of Clark could only seem incredible—a prime example of Kentucky windage. Clark was Netscape's chairman, after all, the only man above Barksdale on the company's organizational chart. But the truth of it was, Barksdale had never taken orders from Clark. When Clark and John Doerr first approached him about running Netscape, Barksdale was one of the most sought-after properties in the business world; ironically, another of his suitors was Gates, who was trying to recruit him to be Microsoft's COO. Barksdale had heard rumors about Clark's behavior as the chairman of SGI: that he was meddlesome, that he was mercurial, that he was a borderline maniac. Before agreeing to join Netscape, Barksdale received assurances from Doerr that he would have complete freedom to ignore Clark's advice, and an explicit agreement that Clark would step down as chairman at any point if Barksdale asked him to.

Clark's email had a secret history of its own. In the fall of 1994, Netscape had been divided internally about its posture toward Microsoft, which was still fumbling around on the Internet and was known to be looking to license a browser. One camp was led by Andreessen, whose position, Mike Homer recalled, boiled down to: "Keep away from the fuckers; they're evil." But others, the most influential of whom was Doerr, saw merit, however transitory, in doing business with Microsoft. "Doerr wanted us to license our technology to them because that would get their endorsement and then everyone would buy from us," Clark said later. "His attitude was that he knew that Microsoft would be a terribly big enemy, so why not try to fool them into believing we were friends?" Reluctantly, Clark sided with Doerr, calling Brad Silverberg more than once and even sending a team to Redmond in December to pitch Microsoft on adopting the Navigator code. "We were hoping to be disarming enough that we could get them to distribute our browser for a while, and then the genie would get out of the bottle," said Ram Shriram, one of the Netscape executives who made the trip. "This wasn't a 'moment of weakness.' It was a perfectly logical way to think."

Yet no matter how premeditated or purposeful Clark's entreaties were, Microsoft's suggestion that they set the stage for the June 1995 meeting ignored how much had changed in the intervening months. At the end of 1994, Netscape's sales were zero, its capital was evaporating, and it was facing a potentially crushing intellectual-property lawsuit by the University of Illinois (where Andreessen had studied and led the browser-building team). Homer recalled, "The scary shit was upon us—that period where the burn rate's high and the product's coming out and the university's suing and you just don't know what's next. It's like the beach at Normandy—the moment things are worst." But six months later, everything was different. In a heartbeat, Netscape had become the fastest-growing software company in history, Andreessen was on his way to stardom, and the company's board had just voted, unbeknownst to Microsoft, to launch the IPO that would ignite the Internet boom.

None of this nuance mattered to Warden. The next day, he returned again to the meeting and hammered away at Andreessen's written account of what had transpired: "These notes of his aren't verbatim, are they?" Warden asked Barksdale. The lawyer then took aim at a chronology of events supplied to the DOJ a month afterward by Reback, which failed to mention the "stunning proposal to divide markets" that Barksdale was now alleging. "If you look at the whole record of events up to the June 21, 1995, meeting," Warden bellowed, "the only fair conclusion that can be reached is that Marc Andreessen invented or imagined a proposal to divide markets and that you and your company signed on to that invention or imaginary concoction in order to assist in the prosecution of this lawsuit!"

"I absolutely disagree," Barksdale said sternly, his face turning crimson. "I was in the meeting. I know what I know. I was a witness to it, and you weren't."

Out in the Valley, Reback heard about Warden's argument and was stunned. Whatever the chronology said, Reback knew that he'd phoned Klein and requested a CID the day after the June 1995 meeting, that Klein had complied hours later, and that Reback had sent in Andreessen's notes the following day. Digging through his records, Reback found a copy of the CID and faxed it off to Klein. (Apparently, the DOJ's copy had been buried away with the paperwork from the fruitless Microsoft Network investigation that had been going on at the time.) Over the weekend, the DOJ turned the documents over to Microsoft. The next Monday morning, Warden resumed with a new line of attack: given the immediacy of Reback's request and the rapidity of the DOJ's response, didn't it all smack of a conspiracy?

"Isn't it a fact, Mr. Barksdale," Boomer boomed, "that the June 21, 1995, meeting was held for the purpose of creating something that could be called a record and delivered to the Department of Justice to spur them on to action against Microsoft?"

Barksdale: "That's absurd."

Afterward, on the courthouse steps, Microsoft's foes gleefully mocked Warden's gambit. Squinting into a warm October sun, Netscape's Christine Varney quipped, "We've gone from *Alice in Wonderland* to Oliver Stone's *JFK.*"

"In my experience as a litigator," Boies chimed in, "there are few signs more encouraging than when the opposition starts saying, 'They set us up.'"

BARKSDALE HAD expected to testify for two days; he spent a week on the stand. When it was over, Microsoft had scored on a number of fronts. It had got him to admit that he hadn't actually heard anyone from Microsoft speak of cutting off Netscape's air supply; in fact, Barksdale allowed that he'd first come across the phrase in a biography of Larry Ellison—an admission that pointed up that much of the government's evidence was hearsay and that Microsoft wasn't the only software outfit given to rough talk or hyperbolic metaphor. More significant, Barksdale acknowledged that more than 26 million copies of Navigator had been downloaded over the Net in the first eight months of the year, and that the company planned to distribute another 159 million copies in the next 12. If that was true, Warden asked, how could the DOJ claim that Microsoft had foreclosed Netscape's distribution channels? If people could still "freely choose at no cost Netscape's Web-browsing software," as Warden put it, how could consumers possibly have been harmed?

Yet the overarching impression conveyed by Microsoft's defense was one of indiscriminate flailing. In the space of a few days, Warden had argued that Microsoft couldn't be said to have destroyed Netscape because Netscape was alive and well—but if Netscape was on the ropes, it was the company's own fault. He had argued that Microsoft hadn't acted like a bully—but if it had, that was acceptable, because everyone else in the industry did it. He had argued that the June 1995 meeting was either an elaborate frame-up, or an elaborate fiction, or a cordial meeting between potential allies, or the wary circling of potential rivals. Lawyers call this "arguing in the alternative." Generally, it is not a compliment.

The government's next witness was David Colburn of AOL. In the industry, Colburn had a reputation as a legendary hard-ass. A stoop-shouldered tough guy with a runaway five-o'clock shadow and an ineradicable smirk, he was AOL's negotiator, its closer, the man sent into every big deal at nut-cutting time. In March 1996, Colburn had engineered the browser war's most famous double cross, in which AOL agreed to license Navigator one day, only to announce the very next morning that it had chosen IE as its default browser, under terms that rendered the Netscape deal worthless. At great length, Warden attempted to induce Colburn to admit that AOL had done this because Microsoft's browser was superior. At even greater length, Colburn insisted that it just wasn't so; that, technically speaking, the products were a wash; and that the decisive factor was Microsoft's ability to give AOL's icon prime placement on the Windows desktop.

When Warden tired of this colloquy, he turned his attention to a series of emails in late 1995 between AOL's CEO, Steve Case, and Barksdale. In one of them, Barksdale compared their companies to the Allied powers that teamed up to defeat the Nazis. Addressing Case as "Franklin D" and referring to himself as "Joseph Stalin" (though he added, "I don't like playing this part. He was not very PC. From now on I want to be Winston C"), Barksdale argued that AOL and Netscape should join forces to take on Microsoft. Case agreed, proposing a "grand alliance" that might include Sun, suggesting that members of the alliance not invade one another's primary markets, and endorsing an idea of Andreessen's—that "we can use our unique respective strengths to go kick the shit out of the Beast from Redmond that wants to see us both dead."

Warden asked Colburn, "A market-division proposal, isn't that correct?"

"I wouldn't call it that," Colburn deadpanned. "What it seemed like to me was a strategic relationship."

Once again, Warden was saying that everyone does it. To which Boies, on the courthouse steps, responded, "The antitrust rules make a big distinction between what a monopolist can do and what everyone else can do." The difference, Boies said, was that "neither Netscape nor AOL had monopoly power."

Apple's Avie Tevanian, by all accounts one of the best minds in software, proved a lethal witness. For three weeks, Judge Jackson had absorbed the assertions and evasions of a CEO, a dealmaker, and a parade of lawyers who, when it came down to it, knew next to nothing about the raw material at the heart of the case—code. Jackson was ready to hear Tevanian's allegations that Microsoft had tried to divide the multimedia market with Apple; had pressured OEMs (and Compaq in particular) to drop QuickTime, even when Apple was letting them bundle it for free; and had wielded the threat of canceling Mac Office to blackmail Apple into adopting IE as its default browser. But what the judge wanted most from the witness, it turned out, was a software tutorial. Tevanian was only too happy to oblige.

The lawyer cross-examining him was S&C's Ted Edelman, who, like a tag-team wrestler, had stepped into the ring to relieve a fatigued John Warden. Edelman, a clever young man with serrated edges, realized he was in trouble early in Tevanian's second day on the stand, when, without warning, Jackson started questioning the witness himself. "What is a codec?" the judge inquired tentatively. Soon the proceeding was spinning out of Edelman's control. Every time he asked a question, Tevanian would turn and address his answer to the judge. When Edelman attempted to pin Tevanian down on one point, Jackson slapped the lawyer around: "Mr. Edel-man, you keep mischaracterizing what he's told you. It's mislead-ing language, and it's not acceptable to me." Eventually, Edelman found himself cut out of the loop completely, as Jackson and Tevanian engaged in an extended—and, for Microsoft, damag-ing—dialogue on the question of tying.

"From a technological perspective," Jackson asked, uttering a phrase that must have felt like Swahili as it left his lips, "what ben-efit, if any, is there, do you believe, in integrating a browser as dis-tinguished from bundling it with an operating system?"

Tevanian told the judge that his people at Apple had done an experiment a year earlier to test that very question. They wanted to see if it made sense to integrate a browser into the Macintosh OS. "In our evaluation, when we did that, we decided not to pur-sue the project and productize it," Tevanian explained. "We determined that it caused confusion for some users in some cases. We determined it caused extra overhead when it wasn't necessary. And there were often simpler ways to accomplish things."

"What you're telling me is you don't think there is any benefit, and there may be detriment, to the ultimate consumer, the user?" Jackson asked.

"That's right," said Tevanian. "We elected to cancel the project because we didn't think it was a benefit."

"Okay," Jackson said. "My final question: Is it possible for you to extricate your browser from the operating system without oth-erwise impairing the operation of the system?"

"Yes—other than that you can't browse the Web," replied Tevanian. At which point Jackson—memories of the consent-decree case surely galloping across his cerebrum—nodded gravely, jotted a note, and then shot a glare toward the defense table.

The Microsoft team wore masks of misery. By the time Tevanian exited stage left, the defense was showing its first signs of disarray, with Neukom calling courtroom huddles during breaks and improvising tactics on the fly. After the case was over, Microsoft's lawyers and its PR people would agree on one thing, at least: Tevanian had been the government's best witness, his turn on the stand, the moment when it first really hit home with them that Microsoft might lose.

The DOJ was well-pleased with Tevanian, and with Barksdale and Colburn too, but Boies had no time for self-congratulation. Next on the stand would be Steve McGeady. Intel had declined to let McGeady submit written testimony, and thus he would be the only government witness whom Boies would examine directly. He was, as Klein put it, "the one wild card in our deck." And while the spectacle of an Intel executive airing the Wintel alliance's soiled laundry in public would have been wild enough on its own, the drama was heightened immeasurably by one stark reality: nobody—literally, nobody—knew what McGeady was going to say.

THERE WERE two salient facts about Steve McGeady. One was that he was exceedingly intelligent. The other was that he detested Microsoft. Whether these facts were connected was a moot point, but they had unquestionably defined his career at Intel.

McGeady had been a Reed College Unix hacker who studied physics and philosophy, never graduated, and joined Intel in 1985, at age 27. Though few people are aware of it, Intel employs several thousand software engineers, most of whom write code which is embedded in its microchips. (As Andy Grove liked to say, "Silicon is frozen software.") It was from the Intel software crowd that McGeady emerged as a rising star. In 1991, he became one of the founders of the Intel Architecture Labs, an operation in Hillsboro, Oregon, that Grove hoped to turn into an R&D facility for the entire PC industry. Yet because many of its projects involved software, IAL was in constant conflict with Microsoft; indeed, the lab was a hotbed of what McGeady called "a whole subculture of Microsoft-haters," of whom he was perhaps the most acerbic. Not long after IAL's inception, he was asked to give a speech on "the software environment" at a high-level strategy meeting at Intel headquarters in Santa Clara. After listening to Grove describe Intel and Microsoft as fellow travelers and another senior exective talk about being "hungry for a new relationship" with Redmond, McGeady opened his speech by saying, "I'll tell you, when I think of hungry fellow travelers, I think of the Donner party."

In the early 1990s, McGeady was involved in a series of increasingly bitter run-ins with Microsoft. Matters came to a head in 1995, when a double-pronged rift pushed the two companies to the brink of open war. One prong was NSP, which was a layer of multimedia software developed by IAL that Microsoft opposed; the other was Intel's support for Netscape and Java, of which McGeady, Intel's chief Internet evangelist, was a primary champion. On both fronts, McGeady believed not only that Grove had buckled under pressure from Gates, but that IAL had been "gelded" in the process. At that point, McGeady retreated into self-imposed exile, heading off to spend a year at the MIT Media Lab. On returning, he was put in charge of Intel's Internet health care initiative—a project championed by Grove, who had been diagnosed with prostate cancer. McGeady's career prospects were fine, but the wounds of the past remained open and raw. He told me, "I really think Microsoft is a fucking evil corporation; they're way out of line in all this." So when the chance to testify presented itself, McGeady jumped first and asked questions later.

From the moment his deposition took place in August, McGeady was "quarantined," as he put it, from the rest of Intel. He spoke to no one about the case except Intel lawyers. He had no idea what Grove was thinking, no idea what the company was saying to the DOJ. ("Nobody even told me I was on the witness list; I read about it in my underwear in *The New York Times*.") McGeady assumed Intel was cooperating, at least tacitly, because it hadn't fought the CIDs or tried to block his deposition. At the same time, however, he had been informed by Intel's lawyers that he wouldn't be submitting his direct testimony in writing. Also, the company attorneys were being squirrelly about whether they represented him personally or only in his capacity as an Intel executive. Then, in early October, McGeady learned that Microsoft was now planning to put him through a second deposition, and that the men from Sullivan & Cromwell were demanding his personnel file, including his performance reviews and salary records. Things, it seemed, were about to get nasty. The time had come to get his own lawyer.

One of the first pieces of information McGeady got from his new attorney was that the DOJ had asked repeatedly to interview him—requests that Intel's lawyers had not seen fit to convey. In the absence of written testimony from McGeady, the government wanted a clearer sense than could be divined from his deposition of what he'd be willing to say on the stand. Sure, McGeady said. A DOJ lawyer was coming to Oregon to attend the deposition that Microsoft had arranged, on October 7. McGeady would meet him the morning after, whether or not Intel approved.

Disapproval would be too anemic a word for Intel's reaction. With its own FTC investigation rumbling along, and the health of its relationship with Microsoft hanging in the balance, Intel was pirouetting on a very thin tightrope. Grove had assured both sides in the case that the company was steadfastly neutral. He had assured Gates, especially, that Intel was doing nothing willingly to assist the government—a claim belied by the fact that Detkin was feeding information to the DOJ covertly through Creighton and Reback. In any event, keeping up appearances was essential here—and now McGeady was about to make a great big mess.

At 7 A.M. on the day of his interview with the DOJ, McGeady's phone rings, waking him, and the voice of his Intel lawyer, Jim Murray, pipes through the receiver.

Don't talk to the government today, Murray tells McGeady; we want to maintain neutrality.

"Nobody ever asked me about that," McGeady replies.

"We don't have to ask you. You're an employee."

"Fuck that. I'm going."

A half hour later, while McGeady is in the shower, the phone rings again. This time it's Detkin, in a state of barely controlled fury.

"You're violating Intel confidences!" Detkin yells. "If you do this, it's a fireable offense!"

Detkin doesn't know Steve McGeady very well; he doesn't know that the best way to ensure that he'll do something is to tell him not to; he doesn't know that McGeady has, in his own words, "a real severe authority problem." So McGeady's reaction is unexpected.

"Pound sand, Peter. This is the fucking US government, OK? Just because you think you want to be seen as neutral doesn't mean I do. This is my reputation and my morality. So fuck you."

As McGeady arrives at his lawyer's office for the meeting with the DOJ, the phone rings yet again. Apparently, the situation has escalated to DefCon 3: Grove's second-in-command, Craig Barrett, is on the line now. Barrett's message is the same, and emphatically stated: don't do this.

"Sorry, Craig," McGeady says, "If the government doesn't want to talk to me, I won't talk. But if they do, I will."

Hanging up the phone, McGeady walks into the conference room, shakes hands with the DOJ attorney, sits down, and starts to chat. One more time, a phone call arrives, but this time it's not for McGeady. It's for the government lawyer—Joel Klein is holding. Not three minutes later, the lawyer returns, apologizes, gathers his things, and leaves.

There it was: Intel had phoned Klein and twisted the screws. Boies recalled, "They said very bluntly, If you insist on meeting with McGeady, then you're going to make us hostile, you're going to make us an enemy. We've been neutral up till now, but if you do this, we are not going to be neutral anymore."

The turn of events was profoundly unsettling for McGeady, who feared that his company was cutting him loose; he was ever more certain he was going to be fired. But the situation was hardly more comfortable for the DOJ. "First we can't get a written statement from the guy," Boies said. "Then we can't meet with him before we name him as a witness. Then we can't meet him before or after his depositions. I put that son of a bitch on the stand without ever having talked to him!"

STEVE MCGEADY testified for three days in the middle of November, dressed in a dark suit and a patterned tie, wearing eyeglasses, a thick gray-brown beard, and an implacable expression. He sat motionless in the witness box and proceeded to pull back the curtain on the most lucrative partnership in the history of modern business.

Before Boies began his questioning, he performed what was

fast becoming a kind of ritual: the screening of excerpts from the Gates deposition. On the courtroom monitors, Boies asked Microsoft's CEO, "Did you ever express any concern to anyone at Intel . . . concerning Intel's Internet software work?" After an interminable pause, Gates replied, "I don't think Intel ever did any Internet software work."

Boies: "And if they did, I take it that it's your testimony that no one ever told you about it?"

Gates: "That's right."

Boies: "Did you or others on behalf of Microsoft tell Intel that Microsoft would hold up support for Intel's microprocessors if Intel did not cooperate with Microsoft?"

Gates: "No."

Boies: "Did you, Mr. Gates, ever yourself try to get Intel to reduce its support of Netscape?"

Gates: "I'm not aware of any work that Intel did in supporting Netscape."

It would take McGeady roughly two hours to make Gates out to be a liar on all this and more. In response to Boies's questions, McGeady told the court that Gates had been briefed many times on Intel's Internet software development—once, at least, by McGeady himself. Gates "became quite enraged," McGeady said, about "the software engineers in IAL who were, in his view, competing with Microsoft." McGeady told the court that at one 1995 meeting, "Bill made it very clear that Microsoft would not support our next processor offerings if we did not get alignment" on platform software—a threat that McGeady called "both credible and fairly terrifying." He told the court how Intel's NSP had caused a "conniption" at Microsoft, which saw the software as an invasion of its turf. He told how Intel's support of Java had been, in the words of one email, a "show stopper." And he testified that "it was

Microsoft's desire that we essentially clear and get approval for our software programs from them before proceeding."

McGeady also told a story about Paul Maritz—a story that gave credence to one of the trial's least consequential but most highly publicized claims. In the fall of 1995, McGeady said, he had attended a meeting where Maritz laid out for a handful of Intel executives Microsoft's strategy for defeating their "common enemy," Netscape. The strategy had three elements: Microsoft would "embrace, extend, and extinguish" open Internet standards; it would fight Netscape "with both arms," meaning both its OS and its applications; and, Maritz fatefully declared, it would "cut off Netscape's air supply" by giving away IE for free.

McGeady's testimony was buttressed by an assortment of astonishing documents, the most explosive of which was a memo he had written in the aftermath of an August 1995 meeting attended by both firms' CEOs. Bearing the title "Sympathy for the Devil," the memo said, "Bill Gates told Intel CEO Andy Grove to shut down the Intel Architecture Labs. Gates didn't want IAL's 750 engineers interfering with his plans for dominating the PC industry." More damning still were a slew of Gates's own emails, which Boies entered into evidence in rapid-fire succession. "We are trying to convince them to basically not ship NSP," Gates wrote after a dinner with Grove in July 1995. "We are the software company here and we will not have any kind of equal relationship with Intel on software." A few months later, after Microsoft had pressed computer makers aggressively to reject Intel's multimedia software, Gates wrote, "Intel feels we have all the OEMs on hold with our NSP chill . . . This is good news because it means OEMs are listening to us."

By the end of his first day on the stand, McGeady had made so many incendiary allegations that Boies feared the Intel brass would intercede—either pressing him to clam up or pulling him off altogether. By the end of the second day, his testimony had taken on the flavor of a software-world *Scenes from a Marriage.* The Intel-Microsoft coupling had always seemed a union of equals. But in the picture McGeady painted, Microsoft clearly wore the pants in the family, while Intel played the part of the long-suffering spouse, sticking with the relationship because, as one Intel memo put it, "divorce will be bad for the kids." ("The kids," McGeady explained, were the OEMs and other industry players.)

The S&C lawyer charged with McGeady's cross, Steve Holley, knew he faced an uphill slog. He started off well enough, using the depositions of McGeady's immediate superior and other Intel executives, as well as a raft of emails, to sketch a coherent counterexplanation as to why Microsoft had torpedoed NSP: instead of being tailored for the forthcoming Windows 95, Intel had targeted the technology at Windows 3.1. "In retrospect, a mistake," McGeady admitted.

But Holley ran into trouble with his next move, a venomous and voluminous attack on McGeady's credibility. McGeady was arrogant. McGeady was biased. McGeady was, in the words of another Intel executive in an email Holley brandished, a "prima donna." ("I've been called far worse," McGeady said with a grin.) He was also a fabulist and a fabricator, argued Holley. Harking back to Barksdale's testimony, the lawyer accused McGeady of cribbing the air-supply quote from a book on Larry Ellison. He accused McGeady of being in league with Jim Clark. He even accused him of being rude about his boss, citing an email in which McGeady referred to Intel's chairman as "mad-dog Grove."

"What is the point of this?" Judge Jackson interrupted. "Are you just trying to embarrass him?" In an act of perjury as great as any ever committed in Courtroom No. 2, Holley said no.

Still, Jackson was curious about Steve McGeady. He had a question of his own, a question that everyone in the courtroom was, in fact, dying to ask. When the cross-examination ended, Jackson said, "Mr. McGeady, to what extent do you understand that you are a spokesman for Intel Corporation here as distinguished from speaking for yourself?" As ears pricked up and eyes widened at the lawyers' tables and in the spectators' pews, McGeady hemmed and hawed. Jackson tried again: "Are you here with the blessing of your CEO?"

" 'Blessing' would be a strong word," McGeady mumbled. "I'm not trying to be evasive, Your Honor. It's a difficult question. . . . I believe that in certain circumstances Dr. Grove and other executives might share some of my opinions. In some cases they would share them privately. They may not agree with my expression of them."

"Are you aware of any instances which are actually at variance with what you understand to be corporate policy?" Jackson asked.

"Perhaps only the most dramatic, Your Honor," McGeady answered. "It's important to Intel to maintain a positive working relationship with Microsoft. My appearance here, obviously, creates a problem there."

And with that, McGeady got up and went back to Oregon.

Eight weeks later, the moment that filled him with more trepidation than any court appearance ever could finally arrived. At an annual black-tie dinner for Intel's senior executives, McGeady came face-to-face, for the first time since being quarantined the previous summer, with Andy Grove. Clutching a cocktail, surrounded by a boisterous crowd, McGeady made small talk for a few minutes and then gingerly tiptoed into the danger zone: "Hey, Andy, um, about that other thing, you know, no hard feelings, I hope . . ."

Grove's eyes twinkled. "Well," he replied in his pronounced Hungarian accent, "I would have done it a different way. But I guess it worked out OK in the end."

■ ■ ■

FOR SHEER drama, nothing in the rest of the government's case approached the quality of its first four witnesses; the next two months were up and down. John Soyring of IBM rehashed the controversies surrounding OS/2. James Gosling of Sun, a long-haired, pot-bellied, bushy-bearded Buddha figure with so many forms of repetitive stress injury he was officially handicapped in the state of California, testified with such low-key candor that his testimony kicked up little dust. Edward Felten, a Princeton professor, contended that he'd devised a small software program that could remove IE from Windows 98—something Microsoft claimed was impossible. William Harris, the new CEO of Intuit, stumbled badly on the stand by wandering out of the land of fact and into the realm of speculation, and by offering half-cooked ideas about remedies, which allowed Microsoft's lawyers to suggest, not without reason, that he was calling for a National Operating System Commission. Finally, an MIT professor named Franklin Fisher, who was a giant in the field of antitrust economics and had worked with Boies on the IBM case, argued that Microsoft had created high barriers to entry in the operating-system and browser markets, and that the company had the ability, even if it didn't use it, to raise prices almost at will—two key tests of monopoly power.

Fisher, 64 years old and terminally rumpled, squared off against the slickest and savviest of S&C's lawyers, an Armani-clad young shark named Michael Lacovara. Lacovara succeeded in rattling Fisher, as he poked and prodded the professor to concede that integrating a browser into Windows was good for consumers because it made computing easier. Maybe so, Fisher shot back, but simplicity had costs. "If Henry Ford had a monopoly, we'd all be driving black cars," he said. "If Microsoft forced upon the world one browser, that would be really simple. That's not what competition is about. That's not what helping consumers is about."

"You seem agitated, sir," Lacovara needled.

"I am agitated. I feel strongly on this point," Fisher said, agitatedly. "We're going to live in a Microsoft world. It may be a nice world. But it's not a competitive world. And it's not a world that's ultimately consumer-driven."

As the first half of the trial came to a close, an air of confidence tinged with cockiness filled the hallways of the DOJ. Klein, Boies, and the rest of the government's team believed the case they had laid out was a powerful one. They felt they had proved that Microsoft was a monopoly. They felt they'd established a broad, consistent pattern of what Klein called "predation, exclusion, and coercion"— repeated market-division proposals, anticompetitive contracts to limit the distribution of rival technologies, all-around brutishness toward friends and enemies alike—that sealed their claim of monopoly maintenance. They felt they had shown that Microsoft had a hammerlock on PC manufacturers; in particular, Klein liked to point to Gates's "OEM chill" email regarding Intel and NSP. And they felt that, through Boies's liberal use of the Gates tapes, they had fatally undermined the credibility of the trial's central figure.

In public, at least, Microsoft's lawyers displayed an almost commensurate degree of confidence. The government was straining to turn the proceedings into a "show trial," Neukom said. The courtroom pyrotechnics were entertaining, but the facts and the law were on the company's side—an assertion Neukom chanted like a mantra. As John Warden had argued in his opening statement, "The antitrust laws are not a code of civility in business," and although Microsoft had played tough, its actions had only benefited its customers. Indeed, even Professor Fisher, when he was asked by Lacovara if consumers had been harmed, had said, "On balance, I would think the answer was no, up to this point." And while it was undeniably true that Microsoft possessed an exorbitant share of the OS market, Neukom believed his team had demonstrated that the software business was savagely competitive, and that Microsoft's position was forever under siege.

That point had been underscored in late November, when AOL announced, in effect, that the "grand alliance" that Steve Case had dreamed of back in 1995 was about to become a reality. In exchange for $4.2 billion in stock, AOL planned to acquire Netscape and then to team up with Sun Microsystems to create an Internet powerhouse aimed squarely at challenging Microsoft. On the courthouse steps, Neukom declared, "From a legal standpoint, this proposed deal pulls the rug out from under the government. It proves indisputably that no company can control the supply of technology. We are part of an industry that is remarkably dynamic and ever-changing."

Yet behind the scenes, the mood on the Microsoft side of the aisle was considerably more sober. As soon as Judge Jackson was assigned to the case, there were those in Redmond who had regarded the outcome as foreordained, and the judge had done little to undermine their pessimism. He had rejected almost all of the defendant's motions. He had repeatedly upbraided the S&C attorneys. He had rolled his eyes, shaken his head, and giggled (along with the press) every time another piece of billionaire vérité had flickered on the courtroom monitors. In November, at a conference in Jackson's chambers with the lawyers from both sides, Warden had made one of numerous pleas to have the judge stop Boies from showing the Gates tapes in "bits and pieces" and instead to have the whole thing shown in toto. "I think the problem is with your witness, not with the way in which his testimony is being presented," Judge Jackson replied. "I think it's evident to every spectator that, for whatever reasons, in many respects Mr. Gates has not been particularly responsive to his deposition interrogation."

Within a few weeks of the trial's opening bell, Neukom and S&C's lawyers had started tailoring their approach, at first subtly, then more obviously, for the appeal that seemed increasingly inevitable. Jackson had given them plenty of grounds for complaint, from the trial's unconventional procedures (the 12-witness limit, say) and the broadening of the case to the decision to admit what Warden called "multiple layers of hearsay" as evidence.

But Jackson's court wasn't the only forum in which Microsoft was faring poorly. Every day, in a cramped room in S&C's Washington office, a clutch of Microsoft PR specialists gathered to review the media coverage of the trial. It was unremittingly depressing. To any reporter who was willing to listen, the flacks flogged opinion polls which purported to show that Microsoft's image remained in fine shape. Privately, though, as one member of the communications team acknowledged, "we knew we were losing the PR war, and badly."

In early December, a decision was made to roll out the big gun: Gates himself appeared, via satellite hookup, at a hastily arranged press conference at the National Press Club. Clad in a brown suit and a gold-striped tie, he delivered a 20-minute speech that hewed closely to the party line. "In the software industry, success today is no guarantee of success tomorrow," Gates said. And, "The government is trying to increase the cost that consumers have to pay for browsers." And, "Three of our biggest competitors band together to compete with Microsoft, yet, amazingly, the government is still trying to slow Microsoft down." Then Gates did something unexpected: he turned to the topic of his deposition and vented his spleen at David Boies.

"I had expected Mr. Boies to ask me about competition in the software industry, but he didn't do that," Gates said. Instead, "he put pieces of paper in front of me and asked about words from emails that were three years old."

When Gates finished his speech, he took just three questions from the assembled throng of reporters. Each one had to do with his deposition. Asked if he would handle it the same way if he had it to do over again, Gates conceded that he might have smiled more. Asked about Judge Jackson's recent criticism of his performance, he snapped, "I answered truthfully every single question." The problem, Gates repeated, was not with him but with Boies. "He is really out to destroy Microsoft . . . and make us look very bad."

On television that night, and in the papers the next morning, "destroy Microsoft" would be the lead for every reporter covering the trial. With just two words, Gates had not only stepped on his own message but provided ringing confirmation of what many in media and the high-tech industry already suspected: that he was paranoid, self-pitying, and quite possibly delusional.

And maybe he was. Soon enough, I would find out for myself.

Chapter Six

IN THE BUNKER

THE WEATHER when I touched down in Redmond was filthy: the sky soupy gray, the roads slick with rain, the landscape draped in a fog thick as porridge. It was January 1999, midway through the trial's courtroom phase. After three treks to Microsoft's campus in as many months, I had started to think of it as a mushroom colony—a damp, leafy mulchpile where spongy-beige coders multiplied in the dark. There were 45 buildings on campus, and a new one seemed to spring up every week. Many of these buildings were connected by a labyrinthine series of hallways and passages, so employees could shuffle from their offices to the company food courts and back again without ever encountering even a dewdrop of moisture. On days like this, you could drive around campus for hours without seeing a soul—and often, you had to. Even on a holiday (in this case, Martin Luther King Jr.'s birthday), the parking lots were jammed to capacity with Acuras, BMWs, and SUVs.

The official line at Microsoft was that the trial was mere background noise; that no one was distracted by it; that they were all too busy cranking out the next great chunk of software. Yet in truth the topic was inescapable. All over downtown Seattle, some renegade artist had plastered up posters featuring a macabre caricature of Gates under the headline "Trust Me"—the first word overlaid with a blaring red "Anti-." One day, in one of the Microsoft cafeterias, as my designated PR handler went on about how surprised she was that nobody ever talked about the doings in Washington, DC, an Indian programmer seated to our left regaled his friends with a detailed critique of the government's technical ineptitude, while a German to our right called Joel Klein a socialist. (My handler smiled wanly and picked at her stir-fry.) Even the hallways were papered with protest. BOYCOTT THE GOVERNMENT. BUY MICROSOFT read a bumper sticker on one office door. On another, just down the hall from Steve Ballmer's lair, was a letter of support from an unlikely backer:

> Dear Bill,
>
> I am happy that you are the Boss of Microsoft and Internet. I want to help you, Bill. Tell the law and the rest of the world. Jesus don't want that Microsoft must pay millions of dollars to the law. Mr. President Bill Clinton has to accept that Jesus is on the side of Mr. Gates. And I think Mr. Clinton knows who is the boss. That's me—Jesus.
> Love and Peace.
>
> Jesus of Nazareth

Among the Microsoft executives I spoke to, the reaction to the trial was a mixture of anger, bewilderment, and incredulousness—mostly the last. "It's totally surreal," said Yusuf Mehdi, an executive in his early thirties who had directed the marketing of IE in the mid-1990s and now was doing the same for Windows. "Whether this technology is benefiting consumers—I just don't think that's a debate. Whether our technology is actually better than Netscape's—I don't think that's a debate, either. Is the browser really part of the operating system? That's sort of absurd; of course it is. Almost all the allegations I just find absurd."

All across campus the sense of persecution was both pervasive and acute. The only question had to do with the DOJ's motives: was it acting out of malice or stupidity? Brad Chase, a Gates consigliere, blamed the "Alice in Wonderland" culture of Washington, DC, and suggested Klein was impelled by (unspecified) political pressures. Charles Fitzgerald, Microsoft's one-man "truth squad" on Java, saw the culprits in Silicon Valley, and postulated the existence of shadowy meetings between McNealy, Ellison, Barksdale, and Doerr (four men whose combined egos could barely fit inside one state, let alone one room) to plot twin conspiracies against Microsoft in the courts and in the marketplace. Nathan Myhrvold preferred a psychoanalytical take, attributing the government's crusade to the impulses of a collection of "very successful people whose deepest regret is that they're not as rich as Bill."

Other executives, and especially those who had already been touched directly by the trial, were deeply embittered. In 1995, as Paul Maritz's 26-year-old technical assistant, Chris Jones had been a member of the Microsoft contingent that attended the infamous June meeting at Netscape. Jones claimed that nothing untoward had happened there. Indeed, he told me that the very idea that he'd been a part of some "Microsoft mafia" trying to intimidate

Netscape into dividing the browser market was "ludicrous" on its face. The Microsoft team was made up mostly of junior-level staffers like himself, while the Netscape side was led by Barksdale, an "impressive guy who had been doing business for a long time." Jones said, "I think the perspectives on who was being intimidated in that meeting differ." Taken at face value, the comment was a telling reflection of the insularity of the Microsoft culture. Regardless of Barksdale's age and experience, Netscape was a money-losing start-up, and Microsoft was—well, Microsoft. When Jones walked in the door, what the Netscape people saw wasn't just a 26-year-old kid; they saw a 26-year-old kid who spoke for Maritz, one of the most powerful executives in the software industry.

And that was how the DOJ saw Chris Jones, too. In a deposition in April 1998, Jones had made statements that the government believed supported its case, a number of which had turned up in its court filings and in Boies's arguments in court. The statements were damaging—and, in Jones's opinion, taken flagrantly out of context. From a 45,000-word deposition, Jones said, the DOJ had lifted a few isolated, ambiguous comments that served its purposes while ignoring numerous straightforward denials that didn't. Microsoft had taken pains to point this out, but the press had basically accepted the DOJ's interpretation anyway. For months, Jones's friends and family had been asking him: Is it true? Did you really do this, say this? By the time I met him, Jones was shaken. "It's been disillusioning, because it's a case where being really honest and answering questions fully did not serve me well," he said. "I'd be happy if there was a trial on the merits, but there's so much other bullshit going on—the PR, the leaks, the Gates video—you can't even tell what the merits are."

Listening to Jones describe his sense of being violated by the DOJ, it was impossible not to think of Microsoft's leader. The transformation of Gates's deposition into a kind of televised water-torture—drip, drip, drip— had been one of the most severe and prolonged public humiliations inflicted on any CEO in recent memory. (Excluding those who've been thrown in jail.) Within Microsoft's executive ranks, the traditional reverence toward Gates was now accented by a new emotion: protectiveness, even a touch of pity. "I feel sorry for Bill," Greg Maffei, Microsoft's then-CFO, told me over a late dinner the night before one of my meetings with Gates. "This poor guy. Look at all he's accomplished, look at all he's done. Now he's being vilified. Not exactly a happy resting place." I mentioned Gates's depression at the end of the consent-decree case. "That was bad, but the videotape thing has been worse," Maffei said. "The fact that it goes on and on, that it feels like it's never going away. Every day they play a new snippet and make him look bad, and there's no way to punch back. It's tough on him because it makes him second-guess himself, which is not"—Maffei chuckled—"what Bill generally does."

I asked Maffei if he thought the clash with the government had changed Gates. "How could it not?" he said. "He's human. No human could go through what he's gone through and come out the other side unchanged."

ONCE UPON a time, not so very long ago, interviewing Bill Gates was one of the great pleasures in journalism—assuming you had a mild streak of masochism. Any reporter required to spend any amount of time with CEOs or national politicians knows what a soul-destroying experience talking to them on the record can be. They are polite and pleasant to the point of inanity. They ooze false sincerity and exude excess optimism. They avoid spontaneity and candor like sexually transmitted diseases, and opt instead to spew prefab answers that carefully sidestep whatever question you've asked. Their primary aim is to avoid genuine communication of any kind.

Gates was never that way. From Microsoft's earliest days, he dispensed with the standard CEO patter and established a rapport with the media that was decidedly more frank. Though Gates could charm and flatter with surprising proficiency, he would also badger, mock, and harangue. His favorite riposte to Microsoft subordinates—"That's the stupidest fucking thing I've ever heard!"—was one he never hesitated to fling at a reporter who happened to ask him something silly or obvious. But the flip side was that, if you coughed up a question that Gates considered sharp, he tried hard to answer it with equivalent insight. "Right! Right!" he'd yelp, jumping to his feet, pacing around the room, engaging in an act most other public figures would regard as dangerously rash, perhaps even suicidal: thinking out loud. Despite the abuse, interviewing Gates was exhilarating.

By the time we met up in January 1999, that Gates had vanished. With the release of Windows 95, a milestone in the history of techno-hype; with his ascension to the worldwide pinnacle of personal wealth; with the construction of the 37,000-square-foot, $30-million lakeside compound he called home; with all this, Gates had transcended the software business and become a celebrity in the broadest sense imaginable. (Scott McNealy once said to me, "What Lady Diana is to *People,* Bill is to *Fortune.*) Transcendence of this kind had taken its toll. It had sanded down his rough spots, leaving him smoother, more polished, but infinitely blander. Now, under assault by the government, Gates seemed increasingly schizophrenic, vacillating in public between bursts of outrage—his attacks on Boies, say—and stomach-turning excretions of saccharin. In the space of one month that winter, he managed to appear on both Rosie O'Donnell's and Martha Stewart's TV shows, where he avoided all topics of substance, let alone controversy, and rabbited on about the joys of parenthood.

The Gates I encountered that cold misty morning was guarded, distant, and defensive. He wore brown slacks, brown loafers, and a white dress shirt with faint brown stripes and his initials monogrammed on the breast pocket. His hair was freshly washed and parted lazily on the side; an unabashed cowlick shot up from the back of his head. We sat at right angles from one another on Breuer chairs positioned next to a small maple coffee table. The tabletop had nothing on it but a jar filled with a dozen identical black ballpoint pens, which Gates would use every so often to draw diagrams for me on a yellow legal pad.

We talked for a while about the mid-1990s, the time frame around which the trial revolved. That Gates had been late to grasp the significance of the Internet, and had then turned Microsoft on a dime to embrace it, was a fact no one disputed—until the court case, when the company suddenly, and for obvious reasons, started peddling the revisionist history that its plans for the Web had taken shape before Netscape's founding. I noted that the first edition of Gates's first book, *The Road Ahead*, which was published in the fall of 1995, had barely mentioned the Net.

"That's not true! This is a book . . ." he started to say, then corralled his irritation and trailed off. "Certainly there were things we missed. We did our big mea culpa in December '95 in terms of realizing the importance" of the Web. "But the Internet—you could still say, Do people get it? Did people know six months ago that Amazon was worth $20 billion? How many people got it? I didn't happen to get it. I didn't go out and buy it, so, darn, that's another thing I missed."

The night before, Maffei had observed that, before the consent-decree case was filed, "in the public eye and most influential circles, Bill sort of walked on water; he could do no wrong." I wondered how it felt to have seen the tide turn so dramatically. "Eighteen months ago, you were universally admired," I said to Gates. "Hardly anything really bad had ever been written about you."

"That's not true!" he protested again. "Let's live in the real world for about half a second here."

I asked him if he felt like a victim of what Bill Clinton had memorably described as "the politics of personal destruction."

"It's overwhelmingly true that the case is misguided," Gates replied calmly. "Was Netscape able to distribute their product? Is that tough to decide? Was Netscape able to thrive in terms of being able to get advertising revenues [from its Web portal]? Well, they were purchased for over $4 billion. Those are the two questions the complaint in this case raises. And that's it. So, clearly, if they've got a tough time with those, they're going to go try and throw as much mud as they can. And there's going to be competitors who are going to show up and participate in that."

Not only competitors, I interjected. Had Intel's participation in the case put a strain on its relationship with Microsoft? "That has no effect on the relationship whatsoever," Gates replied. "You're asking very Hollywood-type questions. These are companies that have to keep innovating in their products. We don't make chips. We're dependent on Intel."

Maybe so, but to see Intel on the witness stand was still rather striking.

Gates's face turned the color of claret. "No, it's not Intel up there—it's Steve McGeady! Don't say Intel! Intel was not up there! Steve McGeady was up there. Was I surprised that Steve McGeady does not like Microsoft? No."

Considering how things were going in court, I asked if Gates regretted having not settled the case in May 1998. "I would have been glad to do a settlement," he said. But, "when it comes to giving up the ability to innovate in Windows, that was something that, whether it's for Microsoft's shareholders or consumers at large, was not something I felt was right to give up."

The distance between Microsoft and the DOJ seemed far too great to bridge, especially when the company refused even to concede that it had a monopoly in the market for PC operating systems. To many people, this position seemed absurd on its face—so absurd, I'd always suspected, that it had to be rooted in a kind of religious doctrine. I asked Gates if he believed it was possible to have a monopoly in the software industry.

"In operating systems, no," he said.

Impossible?

"It's not possible."

Why?

"Because people's expectations of what they want out of the operating system are constantly changing. They want something better. Why have I increased our R&D from a few hundred million a year to $3 billion? Because it's a very competitive business. . . . A monopoly is where you don't have competition. The notion that this is a market without competition is the most ludicrous thing I have ever heard in my life."

MONOPOLY OR no, Windows was unquestionably an enormous asset for Microsoft. (Gates corrected me: "An asset of the shareholders of Microsoft.") And it was one over which the company had claimed total freedom—the freedom to add a ham sandwich, for instance. Was there any limit to how far Gates was willing to press the advantage of owning the dominant operating system?

"I don't know what you mean by 'advantage,' " he said, inspiring in me the brief fantasy that I was David Boies. "It is one of the more proven things that just because we put something in the operating system doesn't mean people will use it," Gates went on, citing the early, failed versions of IE, as well as the MSN client software. "Putting new features in the OS is a very, very good thing. Some of those features will end up being used heavily and some won't. All you have to do is look at the growth of the software industry to say this is an industry that's delivering for consumers in a fantastic way. So, yes, innovation is OK."

Gates hadn't answered the question, so I asked it again, this time more precisely: "Is there any limit to what you regard as appropriate to put into the operating system?"

"Let's say a piece of software is free and it's distributed on the Internet. Then it's available to everyone, friction-free. Is that software part of every PC? Well, logically, it is. They can just click and download it and get it on the PC. So, if we decide essentially to have a piece of software that's free, many, many companies can do that."

I repeated the question once more, since he still hadn't answered it.

"Understand, anybody can give any piece of software away for free. That's just a fact."

"They can't integrate it into the operating system," I said, "because they don't own the operating system."

"Anyone who owns a product, like AOL, integrates new capabilities all the time. Netscape integrated massive new capabilities into their browser—mail and conferencing and dozens of other things. The fact that companies innovate in these products and put new features in, that's a good thing. I can't even think of a scenario where that would be negative."

"But AOL doesn't own the operating system," I said.

"They own their online service."

And so it went, round and round like that, for 15 minutes or so. Six times I asked Gates the question; six times he ducked and dodged. It was truly depressing. The idea that Microsoft had the unfettered right to add anything it wanted to Windows was an extreme principle—but it was a real principle, and it was one that was arguably worth defending. The old Bill Gates would have defended it forthrightly. The new Gates wouldn't, or, at least, didn't. After a year of withering treatment in the press and awful tribulations in the courts, Gates may still have retained the courage of his convictions. But he was flaccid, lifeless; all the piss and vinegar had been drained out of him. In more than an hour, he didn't call me stupid even once.

Yet for all his dismay about how the case had been going, Gates still seemed to hold out a sliver of hope. "Are you going out to DC for the rest of the trial?" he asked as I got up to leave. I said that I was.

"I'm really looking forward to our witnesses," he said. "Now people will finally hear the other side of the story." For the first time all morning, Gates actually looked pleased. "You know, you've got to have faith that the facts will come out in the end. And the facts, in this case, are all on our side."

Chapter Seven
SHOWTIME

ON THE other coast, in the other Washington, the Justice Department had just rested its case and was readying itself to prove Gates wrong. "The next two weeks are critical for us," a government lawyer confided at the time. "Microsoft is putting their three most important witnesses on first. After that, it's all downhill for them—junior executives testifying on narrow, specific issues. The pressure's on David to make some headway right off the bat. If he does, we're in good shape. If he doesn't, we could be in trouble."

The smart money wasn't betting on trouble. David Boies was a great litigator in most dimensions, but his storied reputation rested mainly on his mastery of the black art of cross-examination. Though Boies's boyhood hero was Perry Mason, he had styled himself as more of a courtroom Columbo. As Gates had learned to his consternation, Boies's patience and persistence were inexhaustible; in the IBM trial, he grilled the government's lead economist for 38 straight days. His preferred technique was to turn the witnesses' own words against them. Aficionados of interrogatory virtuosity recalled with awe his performance in the CBS-Westmoreland case, in which he not only ran rings around Vietnam stalwarts like Dean Rusk and Robert McNamara but repeatedly forced Westmoreland to disavow his own deposition. So carnivorous were Boies's crosses that, after a while, the reporters in the gallery took to humming the theme from *Jaws* every time he would approach a fresh witness.

In the first half of the Microsoft trial, Boies's opportunities to shine had been limited by Judge Jackson's rules; the fact that the government's witnesses had turned in their testimony on paper in advance deprived him of a chance to shape that testimony through his questions. Yet with his bravura opening statement, his recurring cameos as Gates's disembodied tormentor in the deposition video, and his crisp spin sessions for the TV cameras on the courthouse steps, Boies had emerged as one of the trial's dominant figures anyway. Now, with Microsoft's witnesses preparing to take the stand, Boies was about to step squarely into the spotlight. Finally, it was showtime.

Microsoft's first witness was Richard Schmalensee, a professor from MIT with wavy gray hair and a well-tended mustache. Like his MIT colleague Franklin Fisher—who, by an irony, had been Schmalensee's academic mentor many years before—he was one of the nation's most formidable economists. He was the dean of the Sloan School of Management and a man Boies described as "a dangerous expert when he's on the other side: smart and polished, practiced and articulate."

In antitrust cases, economists are crucial. While executives testify about discrete events and decisions, the economists, as Dan Rubinfeld put it, "weave the facts together and explain why a company's business practices make sense and are legitimate." Yet despite their regard for Schmalensee, Rubinfeld and Boies thought that putting him on first was a risky move for Microsoft. "When your economist goes first, he lays out in advance a justification for what the other witnesses are about to say," Rubinfeld explained. "If he does a good job, everybody else looks good. If he doesn't, it casts a shadow over everything that follows." It was this reasoning that led Boies, despite having unshakable faith in Fisher as a result of their work together on the IBM case, to put him dead last on the government's witness list.

The DOJ was doubly surprised that Schmalensee was the only economist in Microsoft's quiver. (The government had employed two.) In any antitrust trial, there are two fundamental issues for an economist to address: Does the company in question have monopoly power? And has it abused that power? Both Boies and Rubinfeld said that, if they had been advising Microsoft, they would have counseled the company to concede the first issue, as Boies did in the IBM suit, to strengthen its hand on the second. Both of them believed that Microsoft hadn't done this because it feared that conceding the company had a monopoly would be used against it in future antitrust litigation—a reasonable concern. But if Microsoft intended to fight both points, Boies argued, it would have been wiser to employ two different economists. Why? Because asking Schmalensee to advance both claims put him in a terribly vulnerable position. If Boies was able to discredit him on the issue of monopoly power, Schmalensee might be so tainted that Jackson would dismiss out of hand his arguments on the other point. "Remember, this judge, any judge, does not understand what the expert is saying," Boies said. "What he's doing is evaluating if the expert sounds like he knows what he's talking about. Credibility is key." And when it came to Schmalensee's credibility, Boies knew he had some material to work with.

He began with a string of questions designed to muster the impression that Schmalensee was, in Boies's phrase, Microsoft's "house economic expert"—a kept man of sorts. Schmalensee had testified on behalf of the firm for many years and in a variety of lawsuits, had he not? Yes, he had. In his direct testimony, Schmalensee had argued that Windows' sky-high market share didn't necessarily mean Microsoft had a monopoly, because the "relevant" market was not for operating systems but instead for "platforms." Yet wasn't it true, Boies asked, that in a private lawsuit involving Microsoft just a few weeks earlier, Schmalensee had said the OS market was perfectly relevant? Yes, he had. In another portion of his testimony, Schmalensee had claimed that Microsoft did not have monopoly power because of potential competition from platforms such as Linux, BeOS, and the Palm Pilot. But was Schmalensee seriously arguing that these posed a threat to windows *today*? No, he wasn't.

At this juncture, Jackson jumped in. "Are they making any money?" he asked regarding the rival platforms.

"I would be stunned if they were making a lot of money, Your Honor," Schmalensee replied sheepishly.

If on day one Boies painted Schmalensee as perhaps a tad too flexible in his views, on day two he simply made him look foolish—though the economist did more than his share to help Boies achieve this effect. In researching Schmalensee's past writings in preparation for the cross, Rubinfeld and his team of economists had been startled to unearth a 1982 *Harvard Law Review* article in which Schmalensee had argued that "persistent excess profits" were an indication of monopoly power, a position that directly contradicted his current stance. The DOJ assumed Schmalensee would have a well-groomed explanation ready if Boies asked him about the discrepancy. How could he not? The article wasn't at all obscure, and the argument was damaging to Microsoft, which enjoyed persistently higher profits than almost any company in existence. But when Boies confronted Schmalensee with the article, the economist had no ready riposte. In fact, he had no riposte at all. Dumbstruck, slackjawed, he stammered, "My immediate response is: What could I have been thinking?"

Of all the sentences Schmalensee conceivably could have uttered on the witness stand, that may have been the least advisable. From that moment forward, Boies sensed that Judge Jackson had written him off. In the eyes of the court, Boies said, the economist was no longer seen as the dean of the Sloan School of Management at MIT, but rather as Microsoft's "what-could-I-have-been-thinking expert witness."

By the time Schmalensee's testimony drew to a close, he was visibly rattled. In a final line of questioning that Boies pursued almost as an afterthought, he asked if Schmalensee had attempted to determine how much of Microsoft's profit was derived from its sales of operating systems. Schmalensee said he had indeed tried to figure that out, but was told by the company that "the data that's separated in that fashion simply didn't exist."

"And did you accept that explanation at face value, sir?" Boies inquired incredulously.

"I was surprised," Schmalensee said. "But, to be honest with you, Microsoft's internal accounting systems do not always rise to the level of sophistication one might expect from a firm as successful as it is."

Meaning?

"Mr. Boies, they record operating-system sales by hand on sheets of paper."

"Your Honor," Boies concluded, grinning madly, "I have no more questions."

AT THE lunchtime recess on the afternoon that Paul Maritz was to take the stand, Boies sat alone in the empty courtroom, staring up at the ceiling for a while, then down at the documents spread out before him, like a surgeon contemplating his instrument tray. Boies was aware, like everyone else, that his cross of Maritz would probably be the trial's most high-stakes operation. Absent Gates and Ballmer, Maritz, whose title was group vice president for platforms and applications, would be the seniormost Microsoft executive to testify. His fingerprints were all over virtually every strategic decision under scrutiny in the trial; indeed, it often seemed his name was on more of the email evidence than Gates's was. Anticipating a showdown, Klein arrived and took his occasional seat in the front row, just behind the government lawyers' table. Courtroom 2 was packed; the atmosphere, electric.

For the next four days, Boies and Maritz tangled like a pair of scorpions in a sock. Maritz was a bearded, stout-bodied Rhodesian native who spoke in a clipped Afrikaner brogue. Having sat in on part of Boies's interrogation of Schmalensee, he had a clue about what to expect. As Boies circled him, phrasing and rephrasing, repeating and narrowing his questions, punctuating his queries with the appellation "sir," as if it were an epithet, Maritz hunkered down, dug in, and attempted to hold his ground. When it was all over, Neukom would declare Maritz victorious, trumpeting the fact that Boies had left untouched most of the claims in Maritz's 160-page direct testimony.

Boies measured victory by a different yardstick. In a trial thick with he-said she-said, where so much turned on conflicting accounts of private business meetings, Boies's instincts told him that Judge Jackson would be swayed by whichever side, at bottom, he found more believable. For Boies, refuting every jot and tittle of Maritz's testimony was unnecessary and maybe unwise. Better to drill down on a few crucial points and throw a haze of doubt on the witness's trustworthiness.

One of Boies's prime targets was the 1997 Apple deal. In his testimony, Maritz denied that Microsoft had used the threat of canceling Office for the Mac to get Apple to adopt IE. He claimed the browser was but a minor part of the negotiations, whose "overriding concern" was settling a potential patent dispute between the two companies. The problem for Maritz was the email trail. Boies presented one message after another, many from Gates himself, in which the browser issue featured prominently while the patent issue was mentioned only in passing or not at all. Maritz stuck to his guns. The patent question was so obvious, Gates didn't need to mention it, Maritz said; it was "taken for granted." Boies asked Maritz whether, after scouring Microsoft's files, he had found a single document that described the patent dispute as the "overriding concern" of the negotiations. Maritz had not. Nevertheless, he insisted that Greg Maffei, the CFO, who negotiated the deal with Steve Jobs, had assured him that the first time Maffei brought up making IE the Mac's default browser was during a long walk around Palo Alto with a barefoot Jobs in July 1997—well after the "primary deal terms," including the continuation of Office, were settled.

Having covered the Microsoft-Apple negotiations, I could only shake my head. The day after Jobs announced the agreement at the

August MacWorld trade show in Boston, I interviewed Apple's top executives about how the deal had come together. The dickering had gone on until 2 A.M., just a few hours before Jobs's keynote speech the first morning of MacWorld. What was the hang-up? The default-browser issue, the Apple guys all said; if they hadn't given in, the whole deal would have fallen apart, and Apple would have lost Microsoft's commitment to Office. A week later, I called the very same Greg Maffei whom Maritz was now citing and put the question to him. Yes, he said, the browser had been the late-night sticking point. I asked what leverage Microsoft had used to secure IE's status as the fallback browser. "I don't want to comment on that," Maffei said. I pressed the point. Was it fair to assume that, at the eleventh hour, Apple had reason to fear the cancellation of Office? "Yeah, that's fair," he said. (Three years later, Maffei also admitted to me that although Microsoft had bought $150 million in Apple shares as part of the deal—"We invested in the company when people had lost faith," Gates would boast—Maffei hedged Microsoft's bet by simultaneously shorting the stock.)

Boies then turned to Netscape's air supply. In his direct testimony, Maritz had stated, "I never said in the presence of Intel personnel or otherwise that Microsoft would cut off Netscape's air supply or words to that effect." Boies noted that Maritz seemed more certain about this now than he had a few months earlier, during his deposition, when he had spoken about the subject in less categorical terms: "I have no recollection of saying that"; "It's possible, but I just don't recall it." Maritz said his memory had been refreshed by reviewing accounts of the meeting in question by three Intel executives. In the course of examining Maritz over the next few days, Boies would draw blood on a wealth of topics; but when it came to the trial's most celebrated sound bite, he was stymied. Maritz never wavered in his denials, and Boies could produce no smoking email; Steve McGeady remained Maritz's sole accuser.

But McGeady was not, however, the sole witness to the disputed act. In fact, among the several Intel officials who attended the meeting with Maritz, at least one of them could have corroborated McGeady's account—if only the DOJ had asked him to. Frank Gill, a former senior executive at the chip maker, now retired, was no Microsoft-basher, and he had about as much affection for McGeady as Gates did. Yet Gill's memory of the meeting was identical to that of Intel's chief rabble-rouser. When I asked him if Maritz had uttered the fateful phrase, Gill replied without hesitation: "He said it. Now, in business meetings, you often hear people say, 'Let's kill the bastards,' when they don't literally mean either 'kill' or 'bastards.' I really didn't think it was a big deal." But he was absolutely sure he had heard Maritz say that Microsoft planned to cut off Netscape's air? "Yes, I did, firsthand," Gill said again. "I was there."

THE THIRD member of Microsoft's putative power troika of leadoff witnesses was Jim Allchin. A rangy man in his late forties with a soft voice and a shock of white hair, Allchin was a grade-A geek. He had a doctorate in computer science from the Georgia Institute of Technology, where his thesis had to do with distributed computing—in particular, with his dream of a global, seamless, transparent, networked operating system that he christened "Clouds." His job at Microsoft consisted of nothing less than overall responsibility for the development of the company's core products, its family of operating systems. Allchin proudly called himself "the Windows guy."

The aim of his testimony was unambiguous. He was there in court to convince Judge Jackson that the integration of IE into Windows 98 was real and deep and good for consumers—really good, deeply good. Among Microsoft's witnesses, Allchin provoked the most anxiety inside the government. A DOJ attorney explained why: "Because, to the extent this case is about economics, marketing, and licensing, Microsoft has no special claim to expertise. But technology is their turf. They're the biggest, they're the best, and he's the top guy. We expected Allchin to come in and claim that software was an arcane science, show a slick demo, and run circles around us technically."

The DOJ's expectations seemed right on track when Microsoft kicked off Allchin's testimony with several hours of videotape. The video was designed to accomplish many things, but perhaps the most important portion of the tape purported to enumerate in detail the benefits—19, in all—of browser integration in Windows 98. When Allchin took the stand, one of the first things Boies did was replay that segment of the video for the court. Pausing the tape at the first benefit, Boies asked Allchin: If a user took a PC running Windows 95 without an integrated browser and simply added a stand-alone retail copy of IE4, wouldn't that user get exactly the same benefit shown in the video?

Grudgingly, Allchin replied, "Yes, I believe that's correct."

Boies moved on to the next benefit: same question. Eighteen more times he did this. Eighteen queries that began, "And again, sir . . ." And 18 times, Allchin, his tone shifting from frustration to despair, answered in the affirmative.

Repetitive and laborious though it was, this sequence of questions went "right to the heart of the Appeals Court decision" in the consent-decree case, Boies explained. The Appeals Court had declared that tying together two products was legal only if doing so "offers advantages unavailable" from purchasing the products separately. With Allchin's 19-fold admission, Boies believed he had proved that Windows 98 didn't meet this test. It was, he said later, his most legally significant victory in the course of Allchin's testimony.

The next morning, Boies turned his attention to another piece of the Microsoft video—the piece devoted to debunking government witness Edward Felten, the Princeton professor who'd written software that claimed to remove IE from Windows 98. The Microsoft tape showed that Felten's program had actually only hidden IE, not removed it, and that running the Felten code caused notable "performance degradation" of Windows. But in examining the tape, a team of young software wizards assembled by the professor—"the Felten truth squad," the DOJ called them—noticed something odd. The "title bar" (the line at the top of the screen) of the PC in the video hadn't changed the way it should have if their mentor's code had run. The disputed portion of tape was only four and a half minutes long. Yet from those few minutes, Boies would extract an eternity of suffering—and glee.

That eternity begins simply enough, on the cold Tuesday morning of February 2, with Allchin having been on the stand for less than a day. Isn't it true, Boies asks, that if the PC's title bar bears the phrase MICROSOFT WINDOWS UPDATE—MICROSOFT INTERNET EXPLORER, the Felten program has not been run? Allchin says Yes. And isn't it true, Boies asks, that once the Felten program *has* been run, INTERNET EXPLORER is supposed to change to WINDOWS 98? Again Allchin agrees. Now Boies plays the video. As the narrator describes a PC taking an "unusually long time" to access a Web site and blames the sluggishness on "performance degradation that has occurred because of running the Felten program," Boies halts the tape and points to the title bar. It reads INTERNET EXPLORER.

The courtroom is startled and so is Allchin—also baffled, embarrassed, and knocked back on his heels. He can't be sure what's happened here; but he says that the point still stands, the "performance problem" still exists.

"*You* say the performance problem still exists, sir," Boies responds indignantly. "But this video—that you brought in here and vouched for and told the court how much you'd checked it—is a video that purports to show right here on screen a performance degradation . . . and how it's due to the Felten program. And that's just wrong, right?"

"I did not think the Felten program had been run," Allchin says dejectedly. "I'm going to have to go back and understand. We'll pull all the videos." When he leaves the court at the end of the day, Allchin raises his arm to shield his face from the cameras: the debunker has become the debunkee.

If Microsoft had indeed pulled the videos permanently, Allchin's ordeal would probably have been over. "I had decided not to pursue it further," Boies recalled. "We knew something more was wrong with the tapes, but we couldn't tell exactly what, and we felt we'd made our point." But rather than let the matter drop, Microsoft proclaims its intention to rehabilitate the video, to show that whatever happened wasn't a nefarious scheme but an innocent, if shameful, glitch.

The next morning, Allchin tells the court that an explanation has been found. It seems the PC in the video had software on its hard drive that somehow tweaked the default settings on the title bar. The very definition of an innocent glitch.

Boies conducts his re-cross; hours roll by without a mention of the video. The drama of the day before has lured a sellout crowd to the Prettyman building, and Courtroom 2 is packed and sweaty. (No matter how frigid the weather in Washington, Jackson's habitat is like Key West in July.) Joel Klein is in the house, sitting next to Jeff Blattner, but neither has any idea what might happen next. Boies has kept to himself all day long, and no one has wanted to risk breaking his concentration. The only tantalizing word Klein and Blattner have heard is that the Felten truth squad pulled an all-nighter.

Just before 4:00 P.M., Jackson's favored hour of adjournment, Boies finally returns to the Microsoft video. He starts by asking Allchin if a single PC was employed in the demo. Allchin isn't certain. Multiple machines were used for the tests, he says, but all of them were "Feltenized." Boies rolls the tape and then brings it to a stop. Noting a pair of icons on the screen, he asks the witness, "Do you see that?" Allchin does. When the camera zooms in from a wide shot to a close-up, Boies freezes the tape once more.

"Now, clearly the impression that's being given here is this is still the same machine, right?"

Allchin squints at the monitor. "I can't—I don't know." Increasingly shaken, he adds, "We are just trying to show the demonstration. This wasn't in our lab trying to be incredibly precise."

Allchin's lack of concern for the precision of the evidence he's presenting seems to be the straw that snaps Jackson's back. "How can I rely on it if you can't tell me whether it's the same machine or whether any changes have been made to it?" the judge asks, mournfully shaking his great ursine head. "It's very troubling, Mr. Allchin."

Boies pauses not a moment to revel in the rebuke. He says, "Let's continue with the tape"—and then suddenly, "Stop there, please." Boies points directly to a spot on the screen: where once there were two icons, now there is only one.

The gallery roils with murmurs and gasps. "Holy shit!" someone blurts out from the vicinity of the press corps. Klein's mouth hangs open; so does Bill Neukom's. Jackson's eyes get as big as saucers.

"Now," Boies says calmly, turning to Allchin, "that indicates that something has happened to this in the last two minutes, right?" Pallid under the cheeriest of circumstances, Allchin now turns practically translucent. With no small effort, he musters a "Yes."

For the next ten minutes, Boies gives a performance that is devastating to the point of sadism. Freeze-framing the tape over and over, he shows icons vanishing and reappearing, title bars changing willy-nilly, Feltenized machines that seem to run perfectly and non-Feltenized machines that suffer from degraded performance. Each time Boies commands that the pause button be pushed, the video is rendered one degree more bogus. And each time, its sponsor sinks further into his chair.

As Allchin's torture finally and blessedly ends, the Windows guy hurls himself on the mercy of the court. "I would be willing to bring in a machine here and demonstrate this to the court," Allchin says to Judge Jackson in a tone approaching pleading. And then, more quietly, to no one in particular, he adds, "It certainly has not turned out as a good demonstration."

THE EVISCERATION of Allchin—and the shredding of Schmalensee, and the mauling of Maritz—left the DOJ in a state of jubilation. Microsoft "put their home-run hitters at the top of their lineup," a government official crowed. "And they all struck out."

The defense, meanwhile, was officially in disarray. *The Wall Street Journal* said so on its front page, in a blistering analysis by the reporter John Wilke, who quoted a number of economists—and not just any economists, but avowedly pro-Microsoft economists, culled from a list provided by the company itself—who flayed the firm for not conceding the obvious: that it did indeed try to eliminate competitors; that it was indeed a monopoly. In the Washington antitrust bar, Sullivan & Cromwell's performance was roundly mocked; "incompetent" was among the more charitable assessments. Yet the question remained whether the fault really lay with S&C, or even with Neukom, or whether it actually belonged to Microsoft's chairman. Some months after his testimony, Dick Schmalensee told a fellow economist privately, "The lawyers are not in charge. All the shots are being called by Gates."

After Allchin stepped down on February 4, it took Boies just three weeks to dispatch the nine remaining Microsoft witnesses. A few of them, notably the marketing executive Brad Chase, emerged relatively unscathed. For most, though, the trip to Courtroom 2 was like strolling through hell in a suit soaked with gasoline. Dan Rosen, the employee sent to testify about the June 1995 Netscape meeting, uttered such patent falsehoods that Boies felt no compunction about calling him a liar outright: "You don't remember that, do you, sir?" he asked at one point. "You're just making that up right now, aren't you, sir?" As an email showed, Rosen didn't, and he was. Robert Muglia, Microsoft's designated Java witness, prattled on so incessantly and nonsensically that, with no help from Boies, he drove Judge Jackson into a blind rage. "No, no! Stop!" Jackson roared, covering his face and holding up one hand, as Muglia proferred his umpteenth tortured attempt to explain that a Gates email didn't mean what it said. "There is no question pending!" the judge snorted and then stalked out of court for a 10-minute recess.

Jackson's disdain for Microsoft's defense, never exactly a secret, became ever more obvious as the trial wore on. One February afternoon, before gaveling court into session, the judge offered some words of wisdom he claimed were directed at no one in particular, but whose target could hardly have been clearer. "The code of tribal wisdom says that when you discover you are riding a dead horse, the best strategy is to dismount," Jackson intoned from the bench. But lawyers "often try other strategies with dead horses, including the following: buying a stronger whip; changing riders; saying things like, 'This is the way we've always ridden this horse'; appointing a committee to study the horse; . . . declaring the horse is better, faster, and cheaper dead; and, finally, harnessing several dead horses together for increased speed." Smiling impishly, Jackson nodded toward Boies. "That said, the witness is yours."

On February 26, after Microsoft's last witness, the judge recessed the trial, ostensibly for six weeks (in reality, it would turn out to be 13), before the rebuttals. "Use this time wisely," he advised the lawyers for both sides, who were in no way confused about what that meant. For some time Jackson had been quietly encouraging the parties to reopen settlement talks. Now he took explicit steps to prod them in that direction. At a routine status conference on March 31, Jackson told Microsoft and the government that he was imposing another novel procedure: after the rebuttals were finished, he would divide the conclusion of the case into two phases. The first would be devoted to "findings of fact" and the second to "conclusions of law." By separating the facts from the law, Jackson was, in effect, ratcheting up pressure on Microsoft to settle. Even a one-eyed tea-leaf reader could divine that the judge was going to hit the company hard where the facts were concerned. For a start, there seemed no doubt that he would declare it a monopoly—a finding which, by providing a solid foundation for private antitrust litigants to build upon, would inflict by itself a fair degree of what Microsoft's lawyers referred to as "collateral damage." If Microsoft was going to cut a deal, the time to do it was ASAP, before Jackson had shown any of his cards.

Settlement talks occurred sporadically that spring. Their tenor was never very promising. Although Microsoft was willing to contemplate some of the behavioral modifications it had rejected in May 1998—granting OEMs a real measure of control over the first screen, for instance—those measures were no longer enough to satisfy the DOJ or the states. Indeed, it was during these off-and-on discussions that Klein first informed Bill Neukom that the government was considering a structural remedy, perhaps even a breakup. Microsoft refused to address the topic, which seemed to Neukom nothing more than an empty negotiating stance. The very idea of a breakup, he said later, struck him as "ridiculous."

The last round of talks was conducted in Washington, in June, at the same time that the rebuttal phase was taking place. The rebuttals—highlights included another executive from IBM, who had a diary full of details of threats Microsoft had allegedly made against Big Blue, and a command performance by AOL's David Colburn, who was as sublimely snarky as ever in responding to Microsoft's questions about the AOL-Netscape-Sun alliance—were engrossing enough, but did little to alter the trial's underlying dynamics. By the time the rebuttal phase concluded on June 24, Jackson was freely using the dreaded M-word, monopolist, in reference to the beleaguered defendant.

Yet even with the writing on the wall so garish in hue and its message so unmistakable, Microsoft remained unyielding on the terms of any potential settlement. As the talks lurched inexorably toward an impasse, Klein put forth a proposal for a broad set of conduct remedies, which touched on everything from the pricing of Windows to opening up Microsoft's APIs. In Microsoft's opinion, the plan was too excessive, intrusive, and regulatory even to merit discussion. But the fact that the remedies the DOJ was laying on the table were still strictly behavioral reinforced in Neukom the impression that Klein's earlier threat of structural relief had been mere posturing.

Even with his most trusted lieutenants, Klein played his cards so close to his chest they sometimes appeared to be stitched to his shirt. Yet each time we met, he seemed to inch a mite closer to dropping the Big One. His first suggestion to me that a breakup was in the realm of practical possibility was in November 1998. By the following spring, the word "divestiture" was popping up in our talks with increasing frequency. Klein had embarked on the path of suing Microsoft reluctantly, cautiously, yet here he was, entertaining a remedy so hawkish it would make Kissinger blush. At one of our Saturday morning sessions, I asked him to explain his conversion.

There was no mystery to it, Klein replied. "The nature of the problem and the pervasiveness of the practices in their corporate culture are far worse than I thought," he said. When the case began, all he could discern was "the tip of the iceberg"; it was only after the evidence had piled up, first in discovery and then during the trial, that the full dimensions of the thing were clear. "That's what happens when you try a case," Klein said. "You have instincts, you have views, then you go out and just rip it apart. And only then do you finally understand it."

Klein rose from his chair and walked over to his desk. "You wanna know how you try a case?" he asked, picking up a small pewter mug that was sitting beside a paperweight. He handed it to me and said, "This is how you try a case."

Fixed to the mug with worn Scotch tape was a shred of scuffed white paper, which bore four lines of laser-printed verse—a quote from T. S. Eliot's "Little Gidding":

> *We shall not cease from exploration*
> *And the end of all our exploring*

Will be to arrive where we started
And know the place for the first time.

I handed the mug back to him. "So, if you win the case . . ." I started to say.

"If we win?" Klein laughed. "Get outta here!"

THE FIRST OFFICIAL validation of Klein's cocksureness would take several months to arrive and would be fashioned by an unlikely authority. His name was Tim Ehrlich, and he wasn't yet thirty. A freshly minted graduate of Harvard Law School, Ehrlich was the newest clerk in Judge Jackson's chambers. He was friendly and ingenuous, with a giddy laugh and a gift for mimickry. (His dead-on imitations of the trial's dramatis personae, from Warden and Boies to Gates and Ballmer, would provide Jackson with endless amusement.) At Harvard, Ehrlich had studied under the cyberlaw luminary Lawrence Lessig and had followed the twists and turns in the Microsoft case obsessively. Indeed, the only reason he'd applied for a clerkship with Jackson was his desire to play a part, however modest, in the business/technology/antitrust trial of the century.

When Ehrlich reported for duty in August, he received an assignment that was anything but modest: to draft the findings of fact on Jackson's behalf, and, in so doing, to throw the book at Microsoft. Being fully aware of how the trial had gone, Ehrlich expected the judge to come down firmly and decisively on the DOJ's side. But Jackson's embrace of the government's version of events wasn't merely firm or decisive: it was absolute and total. On almost every key factual issue (and most of the secondary and tertiary ones as well), he endorsed the DOJ's interpretation in toto

191

and summarily rejected Microsoft's. In some instances, he was swayed by testimony that had been offered from the stand; in others, by the piles of irrefutably incriminating Microsoft email. And there was no question that Boies's systematic assault on the credibility of Microsoft's witnesses, not to mention its non-witness-in-chief, had colored Jackson's thinking. For the most part, he dismissed their testimony out of hand.

The judge instructed his clerk to make the findings of fact unremittingly harsh. In addition to reflecting his assessment of the evidence, their severity had a tactical purpose: to create the most powerful incentive yet for Microsoft to settle. Jackson had always believed that the case should never have gone to trial, that the two sides should have cut a deal long ago. His frustration over their failure to do so was mounting, and it was aimed mainly at Microsoft, whose obstinacy he blamed for thwarting the previous efforts to achieve an accord. Jackson hoped that issuing a bare-knuckled set of findings, with ominous and unambiguous portents of what lay ahead, would bring Gates back to his senses—and the negotiating table. As Jackson saw it, a settlement made sense for everyone concerned, from the company and the government to the industry and consumers. The most likely alternative scenario would be in no one's best interest: a verdict from him, followed by years of cost, delay, and uncertainty as the case slithered its way through the appeals process.

Jackson craved a settlement for his own reasons as well. Though presiding over the Microsoft trial had in many ways been a pleasure—he found particular joy in the caliber of lawyering on display before him—he was singularly uneasy about fashioning a remedy. In particular, the possibility of having to rule on a proposal to split up Microsoft filled him with trepidation bordering on dread. "He's not an economist, he doesn't know finance, he doesn't even know much about business, really," a lawyer and friend of his said. "I think he realized that if there wasn't a settlement and he ruled against Microsoft, he was going to have to figure out what to do with this company that was incredibly important, this engine of the entire economy. Frankly, it scared him."

Jackson may have been spooked, but if the same was true of Ehrlich, he never let it show. Three months after being handed his daunting task, the young clerk put the finishing touches on the final draft of the findings of fact and gave them to Jackson for his approval and signature. Released to the public on November 5—and landing on every front page in America the next morning—the findings lived up to the judge's primary dictate: that they be a bombshell. Of the 412 paragraphs in the 207-page document, no more than one or two could be construed as even remotely favorable to Microsoft, while the rest could have been written by the DOJ.

The findings began by declaring the company a monopolist. With its overwhelming and stable share of the market for PC operating systems, with high barriers to entry protecting its share, and with no commercially viable alternative to Windows, Ehrlich wrote, "Microsoft enjoys so much power . . . that if it wished to exercise this power solely in terms of price, it could charge a price for Windows substantially above that which could be charged in a competitive market. Moreover, it could do so for a significant period of time without losing an unacceptable amount of business to competitors."

Then came the catalog of Microsoft's misdeeds. In the view of the court, as a matter of fact, the company had offered to divide the browser market with Netscape in June 1995, and it had tried to dissuade the start-up from turning its browser into a platform. It had employed similar anticompetitive tactics toward

Intel over NSP, toward Apple over QuickTime, toward RealNetworks over media-streaming software, and toward IBM over
OS/2 and its SmartSuite package of productivity applications.
The findings determined, as a matter of fact, that browsers and
operating systems were separate products, and that there was "no
technical justification for Microsoft's refusal to meet consumer
demand for a browserless version of Windows 98." And they concluded, as a matter of fact, that Microsoft had decided to give
away IE and tie it to Windows, exerted pressure both negative (by
making threats) and positive (by offering "valuable considera-
tions") on OEMs and ISPs to favor IE and disfavor Navigator,
and created a Windows-specific version of Java that was incom-
patible with Sun's—all in order to preserve and protect its
monopoly power.

After detailing this litany of sins and more, the findings
addressed the issue of harm. All through the trial, the question of
precisely who or what had suffered as a result of Microsoft's
actions—apart from Netscape—had been raised again and again
by the company and its defenders. And all through the trial, the
government's answers had been sketchy, slippery, and frustratingly
speculative. The same could not be said about the findings of fact.
By forcing PC makers to ignore the desire of some customers for a
browser-free incarnation of Windows, by forcing them to snub the
preferences of others for Navigator, and by constraining their freedom to modify the software to make PCs less confusing and more
user-friendly, Microsoft had "harmed consumers in ways that are
immediate and easily discernable." By undermining the potential
of the browser and Java to create a new model of network-centric
computing, Microsoft had "harmed consumers indirectly by
unjustifiably distorting competition." And then there was this—
the final passage in Ehrlich's epistle:

"Most harmful of all is the message that Microsoft's actions have conveyed to every enterprise with the potential to innovate in the computer industry. Through its conduct toward Netscape, IBM, Compaq, Intel, and others, Microsoft has demonstrated that it will use its prodigious market power and immense profits to harm any firm that insists on pursuing initiatives that could intensify competition against one of Microsoft's core products. Microsoft's past success in hurting such companies and stifling innovation deters investment in technologies and businesses that exhibit the potential to threaten Microsoft. The ultimate result is that some innovations that would truly benefit consumers never occur for the sole reason that they do not coincide with Microsoft's self-interest."

Point by point, none of the findings qualified as a shock. But their cumulative effect was staggering. For years, Microsoft's malfeasance had been the stuff of rumor and legend in the high-tech business; no one knew how much was true and how much the product of fevered or paranoid or Machiavellian imaginations. In the trial, the government had turned the stuff of rumor into the stuff of allegation, and then unearthed evidence to back the allegations up. Now Jackson had conferred on those claims the imprimatur of the federal judiciary: suddenly, legally, they'd been awarded the status of cold hard fact. "It's kind of like the discovery that the Loch Ness monster is real," said Mitchell Kertzman, the former CEO of Sybase who then became the head of the Valley software outfit Liberate. "We've been saying for so long, 'I swear! I swear! We've seen it!' But nobody believed us. Now it's like, 'Oh my God, they were right. Nessie exists!' "

On the Friday afternoon that the findings of fact were released, Gates and his adjutants put on their bravest faces and stood before the cameras. Smiling stiffly, his voice carefully modulated and betraying only the slightest trace of strain, Gates said, "We respect-fully disagree with the court's findings. Microsoft competes vigor-ously and fairly." He added, "Americans should wish that every business was as competitive as the personal computer business." Once again, Gates reiterated his willingness to settle the case on fair and equitable terms. But he left no doubt that, contrary to Jackson's hopes and designs, the findings had done nothing to alter his bedrock convictions about what a fair and equitable settlement might look like. Over the weekend, Ballmer reinforced that message in an interview in *The New York Times*. Assuming a tone so upbeat that it bordered on fanciful, Ballmer described a conversation with his seven-year-old boy, Sam. "I mentioned to my son there was going to be this ruling," he told the paper. "He said, 'Well, I hope it's good for you, Dad. Dad, if they don't agree with you, you guys will appeal, right? Because what you did is all right, right, Dad?'" Ballmer continued, "And I said, 'That's right, Sam.' I mean he's not our legal strategist or anything, but he does understand our view."

But no matter how gamely Microsoft tried to brush them off, when the findings of fact hit Redmond, they seemed cold and hard indeed. Of course, the men who ran the world's greatest software company took pride in being cold and hard themselves. They were clear-eyed, rational, unsentimental. Yet despite everything that had transpired in Jackson's court—the gaffes and the cock-ups, the hints from the judge both blatant and subtle—and despite every-thing that had been said and written in the press, the full grimness of the findings took Microsoft aback. Having told themselves over and over that the worst was surely coming, the company's leaders were still unprepared. Several months later, Ballmer admitted that, despite the cheery familial yarns he'd been spinning for the media, the days after the release of the findings of fact were the only period during the trial when he genuinely felt "under siege."

The source of Redmond's trauma was startling and touching. "Hard as it is to believe," a Microsoft official said, "until the day the findings of fact came out, a lot of us still thought, somewhere deep down, that we were going to win this thing."

Was Gates among those who thought that way?

"I believe he was," this official said. "I believe he was."

Chapter Eight

ROUGH JUSTICE

JOEL KLEIN regarded the findings of fact as "the most damning document in the entire case"—which, in a trial that had unearthed over two million internal emails, memos, and other shreds of evidence, was saying something. Before the findings, Klein had been loath, despite his musings, to reach any firm conclusions about what sort of remedy the DOJ would propose. But now that Jackson had spoken, and spoken so unequivocally, it was time to start making decisions. It was also time to start marshaling the DOJ's allies, especially those in Silicon Valley.

Klein had known all along that when the findings of fact were released, the trial's thrust would shift from crime to punishment—and, as ever, he had an eye fixed firmly on the court of public opinion. If the DOJ was to pursue severe sanctions against Microsoft, Klein would need the backing of the high-tech industry's leaders. Not subtle, clandestine, backstage support, but upfront, vocal, public support: the kind that shapes media coverage and editorial opinion; the kind that changes minds, and moves votes, in Congress. Klein expected the remedy phase to be intensely political, much more so than the trial had been. He needed the Valley to make some noise.

What he got instead was a thundering silence.

The silence of Silicon Valley had been a source of frustration at the DOJ from the very beginning of *US v. Microsoft*. It was undeniably true that Microsoft's foes in the Valley—and some of its putative friends—had been an invaluable source of tips, leads, leaks, and the occasional confidential white paper. Indeed, it was arguable that without this covert assistance the government's case would never have gotten off the ground. Yet the reluctance of the Valley and the rest of the industry to talk out loud, on the record, about Redmond's behavior had been a persistent hindrance. With a great deal of doggedness and even more luck, the government had managed to fill out its dance card of witnesses for the trial— but just barely. And for every executive induced to testify, there were innumerable others with potentially incriminating information to impart who refused to come forward. Too risky, they said; Microsoft could hurt them in too many ways.

As the trial unfolded, some members of Klein's team comforted themselves with the thought that the silence would prove temporary. Microsoft's partners, customers, and competitors might be too timid to speak up while the ultimate result remained in doubt. But once the courtroom phase of the case was over and Jackson had issued his ruling, a wave of courage would sweep across the industry—at least that was the theory. Midway through the trial, a senior government lawyer predicted, "If Jackson comes down big in our favor, all these guys who are too afraid to talk now are going to be beating down the doors and lining up in the hallways to testify in the remedy phase."

To lay the groundwork for the anticipated groundswell, Klein and Jeff Blattner flew out to the Bay Area at the end of October, less than two weeks before Jackson unveiled his findings. Klein had made the rounds in the Valley on several occasions during the investigation and trial. Sometimes reports of his visits wound up in the newspapers; a breakfast at Barksdale's house back in 1998 would be forever cited by Microsoft as evidence that he was nestled cozily in the pockets of its rivals. Other times he kept a lower profile. But in every instance, Klein had maintained his customary demeanor—listening more than talking, saying little when he did speak. Now, however, with the release of the findings apparently imminent, Klein slipped out of his lawyer's garb and into that of a politician rousting his constituents as Election Day draws near. In a series of back-to-back meetings with a dozen of Silicon Valley's ranking CEOs and venture capitalists, he laid out the short-term scenario he believed was likely to take place. If Judge Jackson declared Microsoft a monopoly, a gale of spin would come twisting down from Redmond. Klein predicted that the essence of the firm's sub-rosa PR line would run something like this: Fine, maybe we are a monopoly, but we're yesterday's monopoly, with a stranglehold on yesterday's technology; after all, in the age of the Internet, who really cares about the PC desktop, anyway?

Klein beseeched the Valley guys to counter that spin. For years, they'd been telling him that market forces and new technologies were insufficient to restrain Microsoft's predacious power; now he asked them to make that argument publicly. Klein studiously avoided encouraging the executives to support a particular remedy or type of remedy—structural, behavioral, or a blend of the two. Instead, he repeatedly used a vaguer phrase: "significant remedies." As for what those remedies might be, Klein left it up to the executives to decide for themselves. The crucial thing, he stressed, was to please say something—anything. "Joel is very political," one of the CEOs remarked at the time. "He knows that if he lets Microsoft define the terms of the debate, he loses."

Another purpose of Klein's visit was to solicit the industry's opinions about the various remedies the DOJ was contemplating. Klein was intentionally oblique in these discussions, laboring not to tip his hand. But many of the executives came away with the distinct impression that he was leaning toward breaking Microsoft up, one way or another. "How do I get that impression?" a software boss said. "I get it because Joel only asks my opinions on structural remedies. Any time a behavioral remedy comes up, he looks bored."

That impression was not mistaken. Starting in the spring, intensifying in the summer when the courtroom action ended, and continuing now into the fall, Klein and his lieutenants had conferred in a systematic way with literally scores of academics, lawyers, technologists, and other experts about the best path to follow. The process was directed by Tim Bresnahan, a Stanford professor who had been appointed to replace Dan Rubinfeld as the antitrust division's top economist. In the early 1990s, when the Federal Trade Commission first began investigating Microsoft, Bresnahan had compared the FTC to a dog chasing a firetruck; the pursuit might be invigorating, but what would it do if it caught its prey? Not long before the DOJ filed its case, in 1998, Bresnahan took a stab at answering that question. In a paper widely read in antitrust circles, he laid out a lucid analysis of the dynamics that made Microsoft's power so great and so enduring, and concluded that mere conduct remedies would be entirely ineffective in curbing that power. On the other hand, structural remedies held "the possibility of both larger costs and larger benefits," he wrote. Breaking up the company, for example, carried substantial risks, but at least it had a chance of actually accomplishing something.

What the DOJ discovered in talking to the experts was that Bresnahan's assessment was, in rough outline, the consensus view. Behavioral remedies were broadly seen as well-intentioned but useless, even if Microsoft made no effort to evade them, which nobody regarded as a safe bet. "We talked to people across the spectrum, outside the industry and inside the industry," Klein said later. "And the industry people weren't only Microsoft competitors. They were people upstream and downstream from Microsoft, partners of theirs, customers of theirs, allies of theirs, computer manufacturers, a lot of whom spoke to me in confidence." He went on, "I was really struck by the amazing unanimity that developed among my core staff—Melamed, Bresnahan, Blattner, Malone, Boies—and our consultants and the industry people. There was a real coalescence. By the fall, my clear predisposition and strong predisposition was for structural relief."

TWO DAYS AFTER the findings of fact were released, on November 7, Klein appeared on the Sunday morning news show *This Week* and said for the first time publicly that a breakup was "in the range" of remedies the DOJ was considering. Two weeks later, Judge Jackson summoned the lawyers from both sides to his chambers and surprised them all with the news that he was initiating a formal mediation process in the case and appointing Judge Richard Posner as the mediator. At 60, Posner was a violently brilliant and staggeringly prolific scholar (he had authored more than 30 books, on everything from sexuality to literary criticism and the economics of

AIDS to, of course, antitrust) who had done more even than Robert Bork to embed Chicago School economic analysis in the mainstream of American jurisprudence. Like many members of the legal fraternity, Jackson was in awe of Posner. " 'Awe' is too weak—Jackson considered Posner a god," someone close to Jackson said. "He was of the view that Posner was the only person who could sort out the Microsoft mess. Once Posner signed on, Jackson was convinced from then on that the case would settle."

Although Klein praised and welcomed Posner's appointment, he was pessimistic that the mediation would bear fruit. The gap between the DOJ and Microsoft was growing wider all the time. On December 2, the DOJ announced that it had hired the longtime Wall Street dealmaker Robert Greenhill to help the antitrust division in "analyzing financial aspects of the full range of potential remedies." In fact, Greenhill, whose firm, Greenhill & Co., specialized in corporate restructurings, was retained to examine the financial implications of various forms of divestiture. This became clear to Silicon Valley CEOs such as Scott McNealy and other prominent executives and venture capitalists when the financier paid them a call soon after his hiring. Greenhill indicated that he favored splitting Microsoft into two or three separate operating-system companies, each with the same intellectual property, and then leaving its applications-software and Internet businesses to comprise either one or two additional firms. "By the time he got to me," one wheeler-dealer said, "his mind seemed made up."

As Greenhill made his rounds in the Valley, Klein worked the phones from Washington. Wheedling and cajoling, he appealed to conscience, righteousness, and rational self-interest. "Joel is really born-again on this," one CEO remarked. "He's like Paul Revere trying to rally the troops." Actually, Klein was trying to do something more specific, too. To a handful of executives, Klein suggested that he was looking for a major industry figure to be the public face for "significant remedies"—to make the case in the media that reining in Microsoft required more than a slap on the wrist. And Klein wasn't interested in the usual suspects. "Joel is looking for a poster boy," this CEO said. "A poster boy who isn't Larry or Scott."

Klein's desire to steer clear of Larry Ellison was easy to grasp and unexpectedly prescient. Oracle's multibillionaire CEO was too over-the-top, too unpredictable, to be compatible with even the most informal variety of government service. In June 1999, unbeknownst to almost anyone at the time, Ellison and Oracle had hired Terry Lenzner, the Washington-based private detective known for his work on behalf of Bill Clinton, to investigate the financial links between Microsoft and several allegedly independent pro-Microsoft trade groups and think tanks. The investigation included rummaging through the groups' trash cans and leaking what was found to *The New York Times* and *The Wall Street Journal.* When the skulduggery was uncovered a year later, Ellison proudly claimed full responsibility, calling it a "civic duty." At a press conference, he said, "All we did was to try to take information that was hidden and bring it into the light. I don't think that's arrogance. That's a public service."

Klein's avoidance of McNealy was more complicated. Though characters of more divergent worldviews or political persuasions would be hard to conjure even in fiction, McNealy respected Klein and was amply impressed with his handling of the case. And Klein was grateful for McNealy's famously big mouth. For years, Sun's CEO had been one of a small handful of big-company chiefs who offered a consistent, coherent, and public critique of Microsoft's business practices. Now he was one of an even smaller handful willing to talk (and talk) openly about what ought to be done. Many things could be said of McNealy, including that, as one of Gates's leading competitors, his critique served Sun's bottom-line interests—though its president, Ed Zander, might disagree. What could not be said was that he was timid.

The trouble was that McNealy's position on remedies had been rather like Microsoft's defense in the trial: vocal, energetic, internally inconsistent, and all over the map. After Project Sherman ended in the spring of 1998, Sun's chief counsel, Mike Morris, became a primary advocate of creating instant competition in the operating-system market by dividing Microsoft into three identical companies. McNealy agreed, and what was known as the Baby Bills approach became Sun's official and public position on remedies. Then, at a Sun board meeting in December 1998, McNealy suddenly switched tack. He informed his board members that his preferred remedy was no longer the Baby Bills—or any other form of breakup—but placing a ban on Microsoft's mergers and acquisitions: no takeovers, no minority investments, no joint ventures, for the foreseeable future. (It was one of McNealy's constant refrains that Gates's company was incapable of building innovative new products so it had to buy them instead. At Microsoft, he said, "R&D is a synonym for M&A.")

Morris was livid at McNealy's reversal. "What the fuck are you talking about?" he screamed. "We've been over this a million times! Our position is public!"

"I changed my mind," McNealy replied. "We have to do what's best for our shareholders."

"Scott had himself a little epiphany," an attorney close to Sun explained. "Today, Microsoft is the number one operating-system company and Sun [with its Solaris OS] is the clear number two. But if Microsoft is broken into three OS companies, Sun immediately drops to number four. And if Microsoft is broken into six OS companies, Jesus, Sun falls to seventh. The more McNealy thought about it, the more keeping Microsoft in one piece seemed like a pretty good idea to him."

Klein never had been a great fan of the Baby Bills, but it served his purposes to have Sun endorsing a remedy so dramatic it made almost any other look conservative. It was left to Morris to tell him what had happened. "I just work here," Sun's lawyer said over the phone. "It's one of those things that happens when you work for a celebrity CEO. I can't defend everything he says or does."

Klein chuckled. "I know where you're coming from. I work for Bill Clinton."

Had that been the end of it, McNealy's reputation for constancy would have been bruised, not bloodied. But at a Sun board meeting in November 1999, just a few days after Jackson's findings and nearly a year after his flip away from the Baby Bills, McNealy told his stunned directors that he'd flopped yet again. The sweeping scope and lopsidedness of the findings—and the welter of press coverage suggesting that a breakup was not only possible but plausible—had convinced him that, despite its perils for Sun, splitting up Microsoft was the thing to do. He also floated a new conduct remedy he'd borrowed from Bill Joy: just as Michael Milken had been banished from Wall Street for his crimes, Gates and Ballmer should be "disbarred" from the software industry. "Scott knows it'll never happen, but he can't help saying stuff like that," a Sun executive said. "It's just so . . . *Scott.*"

Ultimately, Scott being *Scott* was what made him an impossible choice as the DOJ's frontman. "Joel would probably have kept his distance from us anyway, because we seem like we have an ax to grind," the Sun official said. "But there's no question Scott hurt his credibility with Klein." A person with ties to both McNealy and Klein remarked dryly, "Joel thinks Scott doesn't contribute positively to the quality of the conversation."

In his quest for a spokesman who wasn't McNealy or Ellison, Klein found a small clutch of enlistees who did contribute positively—and publicly—to the quality of the conversation. One of them was Jim Barksdale, who by the end of 1999 had become a semiretired venture capitalist but remained actively engaged in the Microsoft debate. Another was Mitchell Kertzman, the CEO of Liberate and maybe the funniest of Gates's verbal assailants in Silicon Valley. (He often compared Microsoft to a great white shark: "All it knows is its appetite; when it gets hungry, it eats.") Both Barksdale and Kertzman favored structural reform, and so did the third of Klein's recruits: Bill Campbell, of Intuit. Campbell recalled how dubious he'd been about the DOJ's prospects—about its competence, really—when he was first approached about providing an Intuit witness for the trial. Now, with Klein and his team having proved him wrong, Campbell once again felt morally obliged to "stand up and be counted."

The strength of his convictions was manifest in another way as well. Two weeks before Christmas, on one of those balmy, pale-gold afternoons that pass for winter in northern California, Campbell played host to a sort of anti-Microsoft summit—the topic of which was the matter of remedies. Assembled in a conference room in Intuit's Mountain View headquarters was a collection of some of the Valley's major players, including McNealy, Barksdale, Oracle president Ray Lane, Novell CEO Eric Schmidt (by phone), Intuit founder Scott Cook, and an assortment of high-end venture capitalists. (Steve Jobs was supposed to have attended, but at the last minute he begged off with a bad case of flu.)

In the past few weeks, each of these men had heard Klein's pleas that they pipe up about the remedies, and also his expressions of frustration at the industry's silence so far. For two hours, they discussed what to do about it. Should they speak out? If so, how? Brashly or diplomatically? Collectively or individually? And what should they say? In the end, the meeting produced a fair degree of consensus and a fairly ambitious agenda. The participants agreed that they were all in favor of structural reform. They agreed that, in support of such a remedy, they would launch a quasi-formal campaign with a quasi-official leader—Kertzman—and, perhaps, a staff and a budget. Each of the companies would form a political action committee, to offset the millions of dollars that Microsoft was said to be pouring into Republican campaign coffers to sway opinion on Capitol Hill. They would focus on public persuasion, talking to editorial boards and reporters. There was even an idea bandied about that the campaign should hire an executive-search specialist to rifle through the rosters of former employees of PC manufacturers on a hunt for potential anti-Redmond whistleblowers.

The meeting at Intuit would prove to be the pinnacle of the Valley's efforts at collective action. None of the items on the agenda—not the PACs, not the headhunter, not the staff, not the budget—would ever come to pass; the group would never meet again. Shortly into the new year, a detailed account of the gathering and the nascent campaign appeared in *Wired* magazine. Rattled by the leaks and spooked by the unwanted publicity, the group canceled its second meeting and agreed to communicate by phone and fax only. But soon the phone calls stopped and the fax tray was empty. What had seemed like a breakthrough for Klein turned out to be a cruel tease.

His pursuit of a poster boy was equally unsatisfying. During the rebuttal phase of the trial, Klein had come within a hairsbreadth of persuading Ted Waitt, the chairman of Gateway, to testify. Waitt was young, hip, ponytailed, iconoclastic, and blindingly wealthy. And as he told one of Klein's intermediaries, "Gates already hates my guts." But at the last minute, Waitt had lost his nerve—and the findings of fact hadn't helped him relocate it. Nor had they changed anything for Eric Schmidt, whom Klein regarded as not only clever but fluent in a tongue rarely spoken in the Valley: English. While Schmidt was happy to talk privately to Klein, about remedies or anything else, experience had taught him that whenever he invoked Microsoft's name in the press, one of Novell's products would soon stop working smoothly with Windows.

Then there was Steve Jobs. Back in the spring of 1998, at the end of the meeting where he reamed out a government lawyer, Jobs had made an extraordinary, however improbable, statement: if the DOJ took a serious shot at breaking up Microsoft, he would personally write a $10 million check for a legal-support fund to back the effort. Klein had no interest in calling in that pledge. He simply hoped, now that the remedy Jobs so ardently advocated— one that was anything but "dickless"—was a live possibility, Apple's chairman might be persuaded, at this pivotal moment in this historic trial, to stride to the center of the public stage and speak his mind.

Sure, Jobs told Klein. On the same condition we discussed before: that Andy Grove take the stage beside me.

"It's all completely predictable," a leading Valley figure said. "People hear all this talk about the post-PC world and they buy this line that Microsoft's power is waning, and it's just not true. People have no idea how much power they still exert." He went on, "Ted Waitt needs access to Windows 2000 absolutely as soon as his competitors have it; he can't afford to say anything that would jeopardize that. Eric Schmidt needs access to Microsoft APIs to make Novell's stuff work with Windows; he isn't going to mess with that. Without Microsoft Office, Apple is dead. Dead. Is Steve Jobs going to risk losing Office? C'mon."

After two years of total immersion in the computer business, Klein understood the mix of fear, neediness, and realpolitik that was a by-product of Microsoft's power. He also knew cowardice and hypocrisy when he saw it. The Valley's silence had elements of all these things. It also had a message Klein could hardly miss: when it comes to remedies, you're on your own.

THE STATES begged to differ: when it came to remedies, they wanted their say—and it was by no means clear they were going to get it. All throughout the trial, the 19 attorneys general had wrestled with the disjuncture between their de jure status as equals to the DOJ and their de facto status as second-class citizens. It was the DOJ that determined trial strategy, took the lead in settlement talks, and got all the ink. Most of the time, for most of the AGs, this was tolerable. The mediation, however, wasn't.

The trouble was Posner. He had locked them out, conducting the talks exclusively between Microsoft and the DOJ. For the first few months—when the only news to leak was that the DOJ had submitted a proposal to break up the firm that was rejected out of hand by Microsoft and Posner—the states saw no cause for concern. Then, in early March, around the time of Draft 14, word started filtering out of Chicago that Posner was making headway with a set of conduct remedies, and the states began to fret. The hard-line AGs feared the DOJ would wimp out; the moderate AGs feared it would get snookered. Either way, the states had no intention of sitting by while it happened. To dissect the proposals being swapped back and forth, they needed some high-grade technical expertise. For that they turned to Silicon Valley.

They turned, in particular, to Eric Hahn. Hahn was a former Netscape executive in his forties with a beard and a mustache and a head full of black curls. Since Netscape, he had occupied himself by sitting on the boards of several start-ups, including Marc Andreessen's new company, Loudcloud. Hired by the California AG, William Lockyer, Hahn would serve in secret as the states' unofficial technical adviser. It was Hahn who helped the states understand how provisions that looked solid on paper were actually unenforceable or riddled with loopholes. And as the mediation hurtled toward its denouement in the last week of March, it was Hahn who helped the states devise the hyperbolic set of demands they sent to Posner in the eleventh hour—demands that not only annoyed the judge beyond reason but provided Microsoft with a scapegoat for the mediation's failure.

The states believed they had no choice but to intercede, for they regarded the DOJ's final offer—Draft 18—as too weak for words. For one thing, Draft 18 would have let Microsoft continue folding new products into the operating system. For another, Draft 18 had an enforcement mechanism straight out of *Groundhog Day*; if a competitor thought Microsoft was violating the terms of the settlement, its only recourse was to complain to the government, which could then choose to take the company back to court. The states weren't alone in finding this—and more— unacceptable. Within a day of Draft 18 being transmitted to Microsoft, its contents were leaking all over Silicon Valley. (Lockyer's office was rumored to be the faucet.) Portions of the document were read by phone to McNealy, Jobs, Ellison, and others; some Valleyites got their hands on complete copies. Soon Klein's phone was ringing off the hook, an endless barrage of criticism blaring through its earpiece; the silence of the Valley was apparently over.

Klein assured his callers that Draft 18 was tougher than it seemed—so much tougher, he expected Gates to reject it. "The DOJ thought there were poison pills in Draft 18," one of the Beltway's savviest lobbyists said later. "I mean, they really thought that. But we studied that draft, and there were no poison pills in there. Microsoft should've taken that deal and never looked back."

With the collapse of the mediation on April 1, everything started to happen in a rush. On April 3, Jackson delivered his findings of law, which ruled against Microsoft on three of the four charges—monopoly maintenance and attempted monopolization of the browser market under Section 2, and illegal tying under Section 1—and in its favor on exclusive dealing under Section 1. On April 5, the judge set a "fast track" schedule for the remedy process, asking for a joint federal-state proposal by the end of April, and setting a date for a remedy hearing at the end of May.

No one knew where the DOJ would end up. For several months in the fall and winter, Klein had appeared to be hellbent on structural relief. But given the positions he'd adopted and proposals he'd offered during the mediation, it was no longer clear what he wanted to do about Microsoft. Nor was it clear, if Klein still wanted a structural remedy, that he had the credibility to argue for one.

"How in God's name do you go in and ask for a breakup when everyone knows that two weeks ago you would have accepted so much less?" Gary Reback asked. "You can't. You're screwed."

It was the week after the mediation fell apart and Reback was eating a chocolate-chip cookie in a conference room at Wilson Sonsini. Dressed casually, in an open-necked shirt, khakis, and a denim jacket, he didn't look like a lawyer, and there was a reason for that: Reback was in the process of shedding his skin. No longer a practicing attorney—this was one of his last days in residence at the law firm—he'd recently become the founding CEO of an Internet start-up. This seemed as good a second career as any for a bone-deep zealot. Still, it was difficult to imagine Reback doing anything else for a living besides making Gates's life miserable. (In his office he kept a framed front page of the *San Jose Mercury News* with the headline "Experts Say Netscape Complaints to Gather Dust.") And while Microsoft was one of the things that he was trying to slough off—"I've checked out on that," he kept saying—the outcome he foresaw for the case plainly caused him pain.

"There won't be a breakup now—I can't see it," he said quietly. "Nothing structural, nothing substantial is likely to come out of all of this. We'll get some conduct remedies and they'll accomplish nothing and we'll be back where we started." A number of factors led Reback to this conclusion. The political climate was terrible for a structural remedy: already Klein was being attacked by some congressmen for even considering a breakup. The economic climate was terrible, too: at that moment the Nasdaq was melting down. And Klein had done himself no favors with the mediation. "Of course your strategy in settlement talks is different," Reback said. "You would take something less than optimum to get it into effect immediately; you trade the strength of the remedy for speed and certainty. And you might argue that point in court. But the reality is, with all the leaks, everyone knows what you would have accepted, which makes it very hard to come back later and ask for more."

Finally, Reback laid a measure of blame on Silicon Valley. When Klein had come out to the Valley to test the waters on remedies, he'd found them tepid. When he'd asked for the Valley's public support, he'd been given next to none. If Klein had decided not to go the extra mile for an industry that wouldn't go an inch for the DOJ, who could blame him? "People have made too much money here," Reback said. "They say, 'What's the upside for me to get involved in this?' Which is a natural thing to ask if you're worth $1 billion."

I mentioned that a group of Valley bigwigs, including some from the Intuit meeting, were talking about drafting a white paper on remedies.

Reback sighed a weary sigh.

"Don't they get it?" he asked. "It's too late. They had their chance . . . and they blew it."

GARY REBACK rarely represented mainstream thinking on any subject, but here was an exception. In the early days of the remedy phase, the prevailing wisdom was that Klein would leave Microsoft structurally undisturbed. Dan Rubinfeld, who had left the DOJ's payroll and returned to teaching at Berkeley, thought so, much to his regret. He cited two reasons why he believed a breakup had been taken off the table. The first was Judge Jackson's visible unease with the idea, and the second was the "shocking" lack of public support for it in Silicon Valley and the industry more generally. "We won this great victory—they won this great victory—and then they refuse to speak up?" he asked. "What's with them?"

The states were equally convinced that Klein had abandoned the concept. For some time, many of the AGs had been in favor of forcing Microsoft to auction off the Windows source code—a remedy they saw, in the words of the Iowa AG, Tom Miller, as "somewhere between conduct and structural." A year earlier, in March 1999, at their annual convention in Washington, they had presented a detailed and comprehensive plan in that vein. But when Eric Hahn began looking into the feasibility of the scheme, he quickly realized it was doomed from birth. The Windows code was constantly evolving; what precisely would the licensee get? Making sense of the code would require Microsoft's assistance; how likely was that under these circumstances? Plus, whoever bought the code would be in competition with the company whose programmers wrote it in the first place—not a tremendously appealing commercial proposition. "I spent a week calling around, trying to find someone who'd want to bid in an auction of Windows," Hahn recalled. "I couldn't find a single company."

Robbed by Hahn of their favorite remedy and by Klein (so they thought) of the toughest, the states came up with a package of three sanctions they called "conduct plus": severely limiting Microsoft's ability to fold new products into Windows; forcing it to spin off IE into a separate company; and compelling it to create versions of Office for other operating systems. During their respective deliberations, the states and the DOJ cut off contact with one another, but as soon as the AGs settled on "conduct plus," they sent the plan to the DOJ, unsolicited. The response they received was perfunctory. Up to the end, many AGs—and industry executives, lobbyists, and trial-watchers—believed the states were pursuing more far-reaching remedies than the DOJ was.

They had no idea how wrong they were.

On the Sunday afternoon 24 hours after Judge Posner pulled the plug on the mediation, Klein had summoned his inner circle—Melamed, Bresnahan, Blattner, Boies, and Malone—to the DOJ.

"Well, boys, we're going back to court," Klein said. "What remedy do you favor?"

To a man, they answered: "Ops-aps."

Ops-aps was a diminutive nickname for a large idea. Large, but simple: that Microsoft be sliced into two companies, one (ops) containing the various incarnations of Windows, the other (aps) containing everything else—above all Office, with its near-monopoly on productivity software. The idea of splitting up Microsoft "horizontally" had been kicking around the computer business for years. The objection had always been that, rather than creating competition, it created two monopolies; and according to classical economics, two medium-size monopolies are even worse than a single giant one. Yet once Windows and Office were separated, went the theory, neither would have a secure monopoly any longer. They would begin competing with one another directly and indirectly. Freed from the shackles of the OS, the aps company would have an incentive to work with rival operating systems such as Linux, which would in turn become stronger competition for Windows. And deprived of Office, the ops company would have an incentive to work with rival applications companies. Maybe more significant, both companies would have the incentive and the financial muscle to compete directly against one another. The ops company might get into the applications business, while the aps company might turn itself into a middleware platform—Office as the new Netscape!

Klein and his deputies appreciated the simplicity of ops-aps, its lack of regulatory muddle (no restrictions on what markets each company could invade), and the competitive dynamics it promised to unleash. Yet for Klein, one of the chief virtues of ops-aps was its relative lack of vices. Among the other breakup plans the DOJ studied, more often than not the potential benefits were offset by overwhelming risks. The Baby Bills option was a good example. Dividing Microsoft into three identical companies, each with the same intellectual property and financial resources, might achieve a desirable goal: instant competition in the OS market among the three Windows children. Yet it might also fragment the Windows standard, since there was no guarantee that the children would continue to produce compatible software. "It'd just be Unix all over again," Hahn said, referring to an OS forever hobbled by incompatibilities among its many flavors. Or maybe it would be like nothing the industry had ever seen before. Carving Microsoft into three identical siblings along no established business lines and then setting them loose in the world would be the commercial equivalent of introducing a mutant strain into the Amazon rain-forest—thoroughly unpredictable, and possibly dangerous.

The dangers of ops-aps, by contrast, were minimal. "The biggest risk is that it doesn't achieve much of anything," Stanford's Garth Saloner explained. "You separate the operating system from the applications. These things are logically separable. The applications continue to be produced. The operating system continues to be produced. The OS standard remains intact—you don't risk fragmenting it. There are lots of third-party application providers; they still work with the Microsoft OS company. You get some leveling of the playing field, but life goes on pretty much as before. The question is, does it change anything? Is there real competition that comes about? Do you get any real upside? But on the downside, the worst-case scenario is that you have what you had before except you have it in two companies. I think, in that sense, this is actually a fairly conservative proposal."

Klein thought that was true in many senses. Compared with conduct remedies, which "require a lot of court time and ongoing supervision and playing catch-up," he said, ops-aps was clean and crisp and market-minded. "That's the value of a structural remedy: you take 'em apart and let 'em go back and play in the market; you don't go to court every time and argue, 'It was a foot fault!' 'No, it wasn't!' 'Yes, it was!' " There was another value to breaking up Microsoft, Klein said: it was a punishment that fit the crime. "What we found in Microsoft was a serious pattern of practices and behavior that clearly by any stretch of the imagination was predatory, lawless, and indefensible," he said. "The CEO of a major OEM said to me after the trial was over, 'There's only two people I would say this to, you and my wife: Guilty. As. Charged.' "

Considering all this, Klein believed his breakup plan was not only conservative but "modest." Yet it was about to raise an awfully big ruckus—in no small part because so few expected it. That was the story of Klein's pursuit of Microsoft: a four-year parade of confounded expectations. When he took over as the nation's top trustbuster, nobody thought he would make a run at Redmond; and when he did, nobody thought he would win. At Microsoft, from Gates on down, they assumed he would overplay his hand; in the Valley, they suspected he would eventually fold. But none of the unanticipated turns of events had been more deeply surprising than this one.

Was Klein surprised to find himself here?

"The case came in; it was based on the facts. You put your hand up, you take the oath, and you do the best you can," Klein said. "But did I think I would end up breaking up Microsoft? You've got to be kidding."

ON APRIL 20, in a conference call with the state AGs, Klein revealed the DOJ's plan. Shocked and pleased in equal measure, 17 of the states signed on. (Only Ohio and Illinois dissented, asking exclusively for conduct remedies.) A week later, the government presented the breakup proposal, together with a long list of conduct remedies to be implemented in the meantime, to Judge Jackson.

Microsoft's response was apoplectic. In recent days, the company's honchos had adopted a defiant stance. Speaking with the editorial board of *The Washington Post,* Ballmer said flatly, "I do not think we broke the law in any way, shape, or form. I feel deeply that we behaved in every instance with super integrity." On television, Gates declared, "Microsoft is very clear that it has done absolutely nothing wrong." Now, with his company officially under the threat of divestiture, Gates heaped a thesaurusful of scorn on the idea. It was "unprecedented," "extreme," "radical," "out of bounds." And, finally, the crowning insult: "This was not developed by anyone who knows anything about the software business."

A month later, on May 24, the lawyers from Microsoft and the DOJ gathered once more in Courtroom 2. It was a brilliant spring day—bright, sunny, unseasonably hot. All along, Jackson had indicated that, if the government prevailed, there would be a separate process to deal with remedies. This was the hearing to begin that process. Everyone wondered what Jackson had in store. Microsoft asserted that, given the severity of the government's proposal, somewhere between several and many months were required to depose more witnesses, gather more evidence, hold more hearings. The DOJ disagreed, though it assumed that the process would last at least a few weeks. But Jackson was determined to put this case on its path to appeal as quickly as possible. He'd decided that holding more hearings, in which eminent experts would offer conflicting predictions about the future of an industry that was inherently unpredictable, would be a waste of time. And he was fed up with Microsoft: with the disingenuousness of its witnesses; with its failure to settle the case; and with the recent public comments of Gates and Ballmer, whose lack of contrition was so bald, so galling, that it would play no small part in his decision, a few weeks later, to cast aside his qualms and affirm the government's call for a breakup.

So when John Warden asked at the end of the day what the next step in the remedy process might be, the courtroom fairly gasped when Judge Jackson said, without missing a beat, "I'm not contemplating any further process, Mr. Warden."

Five minutes later, the Microsoft trial was over.

Chapter Nine

WHISTLING IN THE DARK

TWO MONTHS after Judge Jackson decreed that Microsoft be rent asunder, I headed back up to Redmond to see Bill Gates again. The spring and summer of 2000 had been a pair of mean seasons in the software heartland of the great Northwest, and not just due to the judge's rulings. The long-awaited and much-delayed launch of Windows 2000 in February was lackluster. The company's revenue growth was flagging, especially in its core OS business. The Wall Street analysts who followed Microsoft as meticulously as Sovietologists once scrutinized the Kremlin had slashed their forecasts of its sales for the year ahead by $1 billion or more—another reason the stock was taking a drubbing. In late June, the firm unfurled its master plan for the networked age with the blaring of trumpets and the rolling of drums. Dubbed .NET, the initiative encompassed both a strategy and an assortment of technologies that Gates described as nothing less than a "platform for the next-generation Internet." But while everyone agreed that .NET was bold and ambitious, they also concurred that it was not fully baked. For the press, .NET was a one-day story; for much of the industry, a one-day shrug.

On Microsoft's campus, frustration had turned to a sense of defeat. "At the club, in the steam room, people who used to talk about the great things we were doing, all they want to do now is give you opinions about the trial," Craig Mundie remarked. "Even family members are like that. It's discouraging." After talking for an hour about the challenges of taking on AOL with Yusuf Mehdi, who'd switched over from Windows to work on the MSN portal, I asked him if the trial had affected morale. "There's been disruption, for sure," he said, "but there's also been a circle-the-wagons mentality, which is good, in a way." Mehdi paused. "My mom asks me, though, 'Yusuf, is Bill really that bad?'"

Then there was the exodus: for the first time in Microsoft's history, the company was hemorrhaging talent. The bleeding went from top to bottom, from high-profile pashas like Nathan Myhrvold, Greg Maffei, Brad Silverberg, and Tod Nielsen, to browser warriors like John Ludwig and Ben Slivka. In several cases, executives who had testified in the trial—Eric Engstrom, say, or Nathan's brother, Cameron Myhrvold—left the company almost the instant they stepped down from the stand. By Microsoft's count, around 50 employees were peeling out every week, but other estimates put the number three times that high. Some left in search of dot-com riches, others for the thrill of running their own show. Some had grown weary of Microsoft's size and proliferating bureaucracy. When Paul Maritz announced his resignation three months after my visit, it drove home a brutal but irrevocable truth: Microsoft was no longer the place to be.

Microsoft's official reaction to the departures was stunning. In an industry spurred by the sparking of synapses, Gates had long recognized that the most precious raw material was gray matter, and Microsoft prided itself on acquiring only the best. But now I kept being told that many if not all of the big names who had left—men who'd run large swathes of Microsoft when the company was at its zenith—were in fact dead wood; that Ballmer had merrily chucked them out the door. When I asked the new CEO if this was true, he shrugged and smiled. "We've lost senior people who I wish hadn't left, and we've lost senior people where I'm fine, I'm happy, it's OK," Ballmer said. "We've got both categories, and we may have more of the latter than the former." Microsoft's marketing chief, Mich Mathews, remarked to me, "We could lose 40 percent of the IQ in this company and still be the smartest." She said, "All we really need are three smart guys."

When the smartest of the smart guys announced in January that he was handing the CEO reins to his best friend and taking up the title of "chief software architect," some observers wondered how meaningful it was; surely the buck would still stop with Bill. Yet Gates actually wound up relinquishing more control over the company than even many Redmondites anticipated. In short order, Ballmer began imposing new processes and disciplines on Microsoft's operations. And he began systematically replacing Gates's managers with his own team. "Bill and Steve have different attitudes about people," an ex-Microsoft exec said. "Bill likes smart people—plain smart. Steve likes people who get shit done."

Officially, the rationale for Gates's decision was twofold. First, Microsoft had simply become too large and unwieldy for one person to be both chairman and CEO. And second, Gates yearned to

JOHN HEILEMANN

get back to the role he had played in the company's salad days, when he had been intimately involved in the design and development of its key products. Even so, many of Gates's friends and colleagues believed the antitrust suit had played a part here, too; that it wore him out, beat him down, and induced him to seek a less strenuous role. "It's all been very hard on Bill—I mean physically; it literally made him sick," Greg Maffei said. "I think the reason he's no longer CEO is directly attributable to this experience with the courts and the government."

GATES HAD GIVEN no published interviews since Jackson's breakup order, so I had little idea what to expect when I came trundling into Building 8. Outside, the soft summer morning sun sent a stream of buttery light through Gates's picture window. The first thing I noticed was that he looked as if he'd been spending some time outdoors; his freckles were oranger than normal, almost the color of Tang, and his skin tone was closer to ecru than its customary eggshell. He seemed thinner. His greeting was warm and full of good humor. As we settled into our chairs for our hour together— which would wind up being closer to two—it became clear that whatever had drained the juice out of Gates before our last meeting, his tank had been refilled during the 18 months since.

Gates was obviously relishing his new role as chief software architect. In abundant detail and with avid enthusiasm, he described the genesis of .NET, its technical underpinnings, and his role in its concoction. He sang the praises of XML, of distributed computing; he lectured me with verve about "probabilistic input APIs" and "loosely coupled message-based programming." Back in 1995, Microsoft had embraced the Internet, he said, but only as a feature. "It was the most important feature—but it was still a feature," he explained. Now everything would be different. With .NET, the embrace was total; the Net was all.

When I'd mentioned Sun in our previous interview, Gates's response had been as banal as it was disingenuous: "Every comment I've made about Sun had been positive—Sun's a good company." Now I raised the subject again, pointing out that Sun's software wizards, the inventors of Java and Jini, had been talking for years about many of the ideas Gates was discussing today; they contended that .NET was, at bottom, an endorsement of their corporate motto: "The network is the computer."

Gates, who'd been pitching back and forth in his chair like a hummingbird at a feeder, dug his heels into the carpet, propelled himself bolt upright, and flapped his arms. "The most nonsense I've ever heard!" he exclaimed. "But it's not unexpected. The business model of Sun is to sell overpriced hardware." When it came to solving the complex software problems that .NET was addressing, he said, "Sun's not involved in that. Sun has never had anything to do with that."

At the launch event for .NET, Gates had called the initiative a "bet-the-company thing." Didn't it worry him to be undertaking such an ambitious project at precisely the moment when so many of his best and brightest were flying the coop? "Look at the top of this company," Gates shot back. "We've had more continuity of management leadership than any technology company ever." Maybe so, I said. But doesn't it hurt to lose a Nathan Myhrvold? To lose a Brad Silverberg? "It doesn't diminish our ability to do .NET, absolutely not," he said. "We have a team here that is the best software development team in the world. It just shows the embarrassment of riches Microsoft has had, that even without those two guys, we can go and do phenomenal things. But those are great guys. If they want to come back and work here, I'll take them in a second."

But not many of the others, apparently. Did Gates, like Ballmer, regard some of the senior people who'd left as dead wood? "I won't name their names, but certainly," Gates said. "Come on, give me a break. This is not simple stuff."

I mentioned that Craig Mundie had told me, "The trial has significantly diminished our ability to attract and retain people of the highest caliber." Between the shadows cast by the DOJ and the siren's song of Internet start-ups, did Gates think it would be increasingly difficult for Microsoft to replenish its pool of human capital?

"It's a very competitive environment for getting smart people," he replied. "People think, 'I'll go do an IPO and be rich tomorrow.' I don't promise them anything like that. I promise them more impact." Gates went on: "So many start-ups are doing the same things and terribly short-term things. B2C? That fad is gone. B2B? That's in the fad stage right now." For those with limited interest in fads, Gates said, Microsoft retained a powerful allure. "The things we care about are long-term things, tough things. We can afford expensive things. We build 747s. We don't build Cessnas."

AFTER A WHILE, we turned to the trial. To many observers, the most inexplicable of all of Gates's and Ballmer's actions had been the unrepentant poses they'd struck in public in the period after Judge Jackson issued his verdict but before the DOJ and the states submitted their proposed remedies. In private, they had been even more strident, with Gates telling a gathering of Microsoft employees that the company was a victim of a "travesty of justice," that "we are absolutely confident we will win on appeal," and that they would "never allow" Microsoft to be broken up. In the aftermath, a number of state AGs had cited Gates's and Ballmer's public comments as a "slap in the face" and said that Microsoft's aggressive posture had factored in the decision to ask for a breakup. Judge Jackson himself told *The New York Times* that the remarks had "astounded" him and helped make a breakup "inevitable."

With employee morale dismal and the stock price plummeting, Gates and Ballmer must have figured that anything less than an adamant stance would have sent a terrible message to the troops. Still, I asked Gates if, on reflection, he thought those remarks were a tactical blunder.

"You can accuse us of having put Internet support into Windows," he answered. "You can fault us for contributing significantly to the PC market and what that's meant for the software industry and prices and all of those things. We believe that what we've done is absolutely pro-competitive, and it's our right to stick up for that."

I understand you have the right, I said. What I'm asking here is a tactical question. It was a moment of great political sensitivity. Wouldn't it have been better to keep your mouths shut?

The look on Gates's face fairly radiated contempt. "We are defending principles of great importance," he huffed. "Our right of appeal. Our right to innovate. Our right to have an appeals court sit and judge that." Even to mention tactics, he seemed to be suggesting, would sully those principles with the grubbiness of politics.

Another thing Jackson had told reporters was that he didn't think Microsoft had taken the case seriously enough. Had they? "Hey, you should see our legal bill—are you kidding?" Gates quipped. "Of course we took this seriously."

The conventional wisdom was that Microsoft and its lawyers had made a hash of the case from start to finish. They had failed to settle before the trial started and after it was over. In between, they had waltzed into a federal court and tried repeatedly to claim that day was night and night was day, that up was down and down was up, that words with clear meanings were somehow ambiguous—or even meant the opposite of what they plainly said. They had defended a position—that Microsoft was not a monopoly—that even pro-Microsoft economists regarded as untenable, if not downright loopy.

With the benefit of hindsight, are there things that you regret? I asked. Where you look back and think, We made a mistake?

"Understand," Gates said, "that this is an attack on our ability to add new features to Windows, so it's not the kind of thing where you can say, 'Oh, oh, that? Oh, sure. We'll give that up.' " In the end, he believed, the law was on their side. "Every action we took that's been attacked in this case is Microsoft working on behalf of consumers, working in exactly the way we should work."

There was not much more to say. In the face of overwhelming evidence to the contrary, this was Gates's bottom line: They'd done nothing wrong. They'd made no mistakes. In the end, they'd be exonerated. And everything at Microsoft was A-OK. There was no hint of artifice in any of his statements. I believed he believed every word he was saying. It was one of those moments where you question yourself. *Is this man hallucinating? Or does he glimpse a reality that I'm too blind to see?*

Either way, it raised another question: Given what you believe about yourself and Microsoft, how does it feel to have the US government calling your company crooked and calling you a lawbreaker?

Gates stared out the window and thought about the question for a good long time. Still gazing at the trees, he began, "There's a certain irony to being in a situation where we literally have to bet the company on an unknown business framework and a new set of technologies just to stay in any type of position at all, that we *have* to do that, that this is the most competitive market the world has ever seen. The notion that somebody could come in and say (a) we're a monopoly, (b) we shouldn't be able to add features to our product, and (c) throw a little mud in the process—the irony is deep. Very, very deep."

Has the whole thing left you cynical about the legal process?

"No," Gates said simply.

I said I found that hard to believe.

"The law is interesting," he mused. "The US judicial system, like, 98 percent of the time works extremely well." For the first time in a while, Gates looked me in the eye. "This case, in the final analysis, will be part of that 98 percent."

Chapter Ten

THE VERDICT

AS THE old economy gave way to the new, some of the most profound questions arising for public policy revolved around how a legal regime conceived and enacted in the industrial era applied to the information age—if, indeed, it applied at all. Whatever the ultimate outcome of *US v. Microsoft*, the case promised to yield a historic precedent, one that would shape fundamentally the terms of competition in the dynamic high-tech markets at the center of an emerging postindustrial order. "I cannot imagine a more important verdict for the future of antitrust," Dan Rubinfeld said. "If our victory is upheld, it will set the rules of the road for years to come. If it gets overturned, almost anything goes."

Before Judge Jackson handed down his remedies, the appeals process in the Microsoft case seemed likely to be prolonged, expensive, and unpredictable. With the breakup order, what had been likely was now virtually guaranteed. Jackson's decision also guaranteed an assault by Microsoft on his reasoning and competence that would be more withering and systematic than ever. Nevertheless, the gruff old bear in the long black robes greeted the appeals process almost eagerly, and with no small sense of personal relief. By the summer of 2000, Jackson had spent nearly three years presiding over the government's battle against Microsoft—a battle that was not only contentious, arcane, and subject to intense public scrutiny, but that took place on an uncharted patch of legal terrain where old doctrine and new technologies came crashing together. For Jackson, that terrain had always been a challenge and had sometimes been a struggle. He felt he'd done well at finding his way, but as the trial dragged on, some doubts crept in. "I have been in splendid isolation on this case long enough," the judge told *The New York Times* in March, in an interview published after the trial was over. "I would welcome another mind studying my work product to see if I am correct or wrongheaded," he said. "I want to bring in other minds as quickly as possible."

In April, at a conference in his chambers with the lawyers for both sides, Jackson identified precisely the minds he had in mind: those encased in the skulls of the nine Supreme Court Justices. Under the auspices of an obscure federal law called the Antitrust Expediting Act, antitrust cases "of general public importance in the administration of justice" could be appealed directly to the High Court for a ruling. In the 26 years since the Expediting Act was passed, the government had invoked it on only two occasions, both times in its litigation against AT&T. Jackson had no doubt that the Microsoft case was a matter of great public import, with implications for the national (and perhaps global) economy, the stock market, the technology sector, and the business world at large. And he had no doubt that the questions surrounding a breakup of Gates's company were every bit as urgent as those surrounding the dismantlement of Ma Bell had been in 1970s and 1980s. If ever there was a case for which the Expediting Act seemed to have been written, Jackson believed, *US v. Microsoft* was it.

Of course, Jackson had another motive for wanting the appeal to go straight to the top: it would circumvent the Appeals Court, which had so rudely overturned his decision in the consent-decree case. On this issue, as had been the case so often during the trial, Jackson and the government were in perfect concurrence. And, once again, they were at odds with Redmond. Microsoft's official position was that, especially considering the gravity of the proposed remedies, it was entitled to pursue the appeals process through its full and normal course. But, in fact, Gates and his allies wanted to wind up in the Appeals Court for precisely the reason that Jackson, the DOJ, and the states did not: because they all regarded that venue, with good reason, as hospitable to Microsoft's arguments.

In the weeks after the breakup order, the parties engaged in a flurry of feverish and sometimes inscrutable legal maneuvering. There were two matters at stake. The first was Microsoft's desire to have the remedies stayed. According to Judge Jackson's order, the divestiture was automatically put on hold until all the appeals in the case were complete. The conduct remedies, however, would kick in a few weeks hence. Microsoft considered the behavioral provisions intolerable. Included were many items the DOJ had sought over the years in the settlement talks, such as a uniform price list for Windows, a ban on exclusive contracts, opening up the Windows APIs, restrictions on bundling, and granting OEMs some freedom to alter Windows. As a formality, expecting nothing to come of it, the company petitioned Jackson to stay the conduct remedies, and then went over his head to ask the Appeals Court to do the same. But on June 20, without any warning, Jackson announced he was staying his own order—an order he'd signed only two weeks earlier. On the Microsoft campus, there was over-joyed befuddlement; at the DOJ, downcast confusion. In both places, people wondered if the judge was senile.

As usual, Judge Jackson proved himself more cagey than crack-pot. His handling of the remedy process, it was generally agreed, had been the most glaringly dubious of his actions in the trial. Microsoft complained that Jackson had denied the company due process. And even among antitrust experts who sided with the government, there was widespread incredulity that he had devoted a single half-day hearing to the monumentally complex issue of hacking Microsoft in two. "I have nothing good to say about it," commented William Kovacic, a law professor and antitrust spe-cialist at George Washington University. "It was a tremendously glib way to handle a very serious process." But now Judge Jackson confounded his critics. If no remedies of any kind would be imposed until after a higher court ruled, how could Microsoft or anyone else moan about a lack of due process?

The second legal tussle was over the Supreme Court. In July and August, respectively, Microsoft and the DOJ filed briefs with the Court on the question of a direct appeal. The government's argument rested on the idea that, given the headsnapping pace of the software industry, time was of the essence; a drawn-out appeals process would allow an unconstrained Microsoft to grow only more dominant. Microsoft's argument was based on the expectation that its appeal would be so sweeping and multifarious—challenging Jackson's findings of fact, his interpretations of law, the procedures he used, and the evidence he accepted—that it would "impose an extraordinary burden on this Court." Apparently, this Court agreed. In September, it turned down the DOJ's request, and, in effect, handed the case over to the Appeals Court.

According to the schedule the Appeals Court laid out, oral arguments would take place early in 2001; a ruling was likely sometime in the spring. After that, most antitrust aficionados assumed that one of the two parties would send the case bouncing back up the Supreme Court's steps. Others speculated that the new Department of Justice, appointed by the new Republican president, George W. Bush, would choose not to pursue the case further after the Appeals Court ruled, especially if its ruling favored Microsoft. But although such an action would not be unprecedented, it would be unusual—and probably irrelevant. All that would be needed to keep the case alive was the presence of one sufficiently determined (or demented) state attorney general. Unless Gates could somehow orchestrate a unanimous anti-incumbent sweep through the nation's statehouses, the appeals process was likely to continue to the point of its exhaustion.

In the higher courts, Microsoft's claims would be many and varied, but at the core of its appeals strategy would be its arguments on tying. Long after Jackson had found the company guilty of monopoly maintenance, and even longer after the DOJ had put that charge at the center of the lawsuit, Microsoft continued to insist that the complaint about the integration of IE into the operating system remained the true linchpin of the government's case and Jackson's ruling. In August, Gates informed me in no uncertain terms that, despite all the spin to the contrary, *US v. Microsoft* was still little more than a browser case, if you looked at it carefully. Of the three counts of violating the Sherman Act on which

Jackson had found Microsoft culpable, one was illegal tying itself; another was attempted monopolization of the browser market, which the firm was said to have carried out primarily by tying IE to Windows; and the third was monopoly maintenance—a broader count, Gates allowed, but one in which the company's supposedly predatory product design decisions were a large factor. If Microsoft won the tying argument on appeal, Gates believed that it would severely undercut, if not completely obliterate, the rest of the ruling against the company in one fell swoop.

Gates's legal interpretation struck many antitrust experts as excessively hopeful in tone and as something of a stretch in substance. Yet most of those same experts agreed that tying was the area in which Jackson and the government were most vulnerable on appeal. (Even Joel Klein privately admitted as much.) They agreed as well that the tying and attempted monopolization claims were indeed bound up together legally, and that if the former fell, the latter would be in jeopardy. And they agreed that if Microsoft succeeded in chipping away at the ruling against it—if it could knock out even one of the counts against it, and certainly if it could knock out two—the justification for breaking up the company would become increasingly tenuous. In legal circles anywhere outside Redmond, the notion that the appeals process would produce an across-the-board reversal was seen as highly implausible. But the possibility that Gates and his legal team would extract the company from the jaws of divestiture seemed not just plausible but reasonably likely.

What if the efforts at extraction failed? What if the antitrust experts were wrong—as they often had been in analyzing the Microsoft case—and Judge Jackson's ruling and remedies survived intact? The picture then was far more opaque. For all the scorn heaped upon it, Jackson's refusal to engage in lengthy remedy proceedings was rooted in at least one home truth: nobody really had a clue what a breakup would mean. In Silicon Valley, there was a plethora of sensible, intelligent executives who thought the government was right: that halving Microsoft would unleash competition and let innovation reign. But there were also plenty who believed the opposite: that the industry would simply be saddled with two Microsoft monopolies instead of one. There were many who argued that the applications company would flourish while the OS company withered; there were others who said that both would be doomed. Would consumers benefit from a breakup or would they suffer? Would shareholders prosper or would they get hammered? For every two questions, there were at least five theories. Putting aside prognostication, only one thing was certain: a breakup would mean the end of Microsoft as we knew it.

Yet all the speculation about the effects of a breakup obscured a simple but staggering fact. We were already witnessing the end of Microsoft as we'd known it. For three years, Gates and his company had been caught in a pincers. Pressing in from one side was a technological shift more sweeping than any since the rise of the PC: the Internet. And pressing in from the other was a menace more threatening than anything Microsoft had ever encountered in the world of business: the United States government. For a lesser company, either of these forces alone would surely have spelled ruin. But it took both, working in devilish harmony, to put Microsoft on the path to a new identity.

On Microsoft's campus they could sense the transformation, but they struggled for the words to describe it with precision. When I visited in June 2000, the people I spoke to were more apprehensive about the future than I had ever seen them. With the company turning 25 years old that summer, middle age was encroaching; could Microsoft stay vital? "The question is: Do we recede or do we maintain our leadership?" asked Craig Mundie.

"Or are we superseded by another company that rises up and takes leadership? People say .NET is a 'bet the company' thing. But companies don't roll over and die. The question is whether we become just another company."

When Nathan Myhrvold still worked at Microsoft, he had an expression for just such occasions—"putting a name to the nameless dread." After spending some time with Mundie, though, it began to become clear that the dread Microsoft was feeling had a name after all. "Either Microsoft will stay Microsoft or it will become IBM," he said. "That's just my opinion. But I think those are the stakes involved in this transition."

At the dawn of the PC era, when Big Blue's power was as yet unchallenged, the personal-computing revolution had presented the company with a choice: Resist it, ignore it, or get with the program. IBM opted to get with it—or at least to make the effort—and for several years it dominated the market. But the forces of change unleashed by the PC were too swift, democratic, and decentralizing to contain. At the end of 2000, IBM was still the biggest manufacturer of mainframe computers in the world. It had a stock market value of more than $150 billion. It had happy shareholders, happy customers, happy employees. Yet few people feared it or followed it; nobody considered Big Blue a leader anymore.

Microsoft at the beginning of the new century was on an eerily similar trajectory. Just as IBM had embraced the PC, so Redmond was laboring mightily to embrace the Net. Yet in the glow of the efflorescent Internet economy, Microsoft's position seemed, if not fragile, then increasingly peripheral. The real estate it controlled, the PC desktop, remained the most valuable territory on the digital map. But, as everyone could see, the universe of computing was expanding and exploding, while the desktop seemed to be shrinking in strategic importance.

Andy Grove found the parallel compelling. "For a long time in the 1980s, IBM was everything to Intel," he explained. "We thought about them constantly, lived and died by their whim. Then around 1990, I woke up one day and it wasn't so anymore. It wasn't some momentous event. And now it was Microsoft who we thought about all the time. Maybe this is happening again—only this time, instead of Microsoft being replaced by another company, it's being replaced by the Internet, by a whole bunch of things happening all at once."

Creeping giantism had begun to take hold at Gates's firm, too. Microsoft's goal had long been to retain its agility even as it grew—to be "the smallest big company around," as Brad Chase put it. Yet by late 2000, Microsoft had become a *very* big company, with 40,000 employees worldwide. Though that 40,000 included the largest concentration of skilled coders anywhere on the planet, the culture of the company had begun to smell as much of marketing and sales as it did of technology—a distinctly IBM-ish aroma. At the same time, the sheer scale of the software endeavors into which Gates had plunged Microsoft's programmers had a certain whiff of old IBM as well. The Gates who boasted to me about how Microsoft "builds 747s" was the same man who, in the 1980s, had mocked Big Blue's programmers by saying that IBM's motto was: "Building the world's heaviest airplane."

Meanwhile, Microsoft's well-known insularity had taken on a new dimension. In their heyday, Gates and Ballmer were relentlessly in touch with the industry they sought to rule. On the floors of trade shows, in the hotel ballrooms at high-tech conferences, they picked brains, probed for clues, and tested their assumptions against the prevailing wisdom. No longer. Hemmed in by his wealth and fame, Gates attended few industry events anymore, and when he did, his appearances were scripted; spontaneous exchanges were strictly verboten. Even among his fellow info-tycoons at Herb Allen's annual schmoozefest in Sun Valley, Gates was known to keep largely to himself. (Kay Graham and Warren Buffett were the only guests with whom he routinely socialized.) As for Ballmer, when the new CEO was invited in the summer of 2000 to speak at one of the Internet industry's preeminent conferences, the organizers were rebuffed with a messsage from his handlers: "Steve says he doesn't speak at conferences where he doesn't have any customers."

There was one other parallel between Microsoft and IBM, and the irony here was thick. IBM's entanglement with the government had paralyzed the company. By doing everything in his power to avoid such paralysis, Gates brought the government slamming down on Microsoft. The demoralized employees, the slumping stock price, the cloud of uncertainty hanging over Redmond—in a way, all of it was due to Gates's IBM phobia. By trying to avoid Big Blue's fate, Gates had instead done much to guarantee it.

Not surprisingly, the suggestion that Microsoft might wind up as the new IBM was one that Gates and Ballmer were unwilling to countenance. When I asked Ballmer if it would be a bad fate to be perceived that way in five or ten years—as successful and solid but no longer dominant—he nodded his head in violent agreement. "Yes," he said. "Terrible? No. Bad? Yes." When I asked Gates the same question, he answered as emphatically: "Absolutely."

Gates imagined for himself a rosier future. Though he told me he could envision a day—in his fifties—when he would no longer be Microsoft's chairman, he was "excited," he said, that "in these next couple years, I'll get to do some of my most interesting work." To the extent he admitted his reputation had been muddied, he assumed, like John D. Rockefeller, the plutocrat with whom he was

so often compared, that he would be vindicated. But where Rockefeller had believed his vindication would be dispensed by history
and in heaven, Gates expected to receive his very shortly—and
here on earth. According to polls, he remained one of the most
admired figures in the world of business. And his $21 billion char-
itable foundation had made him a hero in the world of philanthropy. The only thing missing was the higher court reversal he so
manifestly considered his due.

Yet no matter how favorable the courts' final verdict, it would
never provide the kind of satisfaction for which Gates yearned.
"Vindication will be bittersweet," a Microsoft official said ruefully
one day, reflecting on the tumultuous events of the past few years.
"The company has suffered too much. Before, people thought the
world of us. That we were great innovators. That we were this great
engine of the new economy. Now, either the decision stands, in
which case people think we're criminals, or the decision is overturned, and people think we somehow got away with something.
No vindication will erase that stain."

Truer words were never spoken. Before the Microsoft trial
began, Gates was more than a high-tech hero; he was the pristine
embodiment of the high-tech myth. At an impossibly young age,
he'd come out of nowhere, consumed with ideas and a pure burn-
ing passion. He had launched a company that unleashed an industry, and then led that industry as it transformed an economy. For a
long time, Gates represented everything that was inspiring about
this protean phenomenon taking shape in our midst—its fresh-
ness and its ambition, its sense of possibility and its connection to
the future. But like a figure lifted from classical tragedy, Gates
sowed the seeds of his own undoing. He created a company that
reflected his image and fostered a culture that fed his sense of
omnipotence. He mastered a business that rewarded farsighted-

ness, but he failed to develop his peripheral vision. In his arrogance he lost whatever perspective he once had, and in his monomania he was unwise to the ways of the world. He began his journey as an aspiring god, an illusion his universe nurtured and sustained. When his reckoning came, it was shocking and final—and it seemed somehow ordained by the ages. For the wreckage of the trial revealed that Gates was mortal.

Acknowledgments

The last thing I ever intended was to write a book about Bill Gates or the Microsoft trial. Well, maybe not the last—but it certainly wasn't the original plan. In the fall of 1997, I started work on a book about Silicon Valley, which had as its focus a number of characters and companies that either competed or cooperated (or some combustible mixture of the two) with Microsoft. After the Justice Department launched its lawsuit a few months later, I covered the case closely, obsessively, but what interested me mainly was the window it provided on the machinations of the Valley and the fact that it seemed a watershed in the relationship between the technology industry and the federal government. It wasn't until the summer of 2000 that it finally dawned on me—with the help of Judge Jackson's breakup order and the wise counsel of several people thanked below—that the most compelling thing about the Microsoft trial was, hello, Microsoft; and that it might make sense to put aside temporarily the slow-motion marathon that was my Silicon Valley book and get this story down on paper.

Any attempt to dig out the story behind a story as public and voluminously chronicled as the Microsoft trial depends heavily on the trust, candor, and, above all, patience of the players involved. Although my reporting was informed by the newspaper and magazine coverage of the case—much of it excellent, especially that of *The Wall Street Journal*'s John Wilke and *Fortune*'s Joe Nocera—I relied primarily on firsthand interviews. Over the course of nearly three years, almost every person named in the preceding pages agreed to talk to me, with many of the central characters sitting for repeated interviews and follow-ups by telephone. There were also dozens who spoke to me but remain unnamed, often at their request. In all, the book is based on more than 400 interviews with more than 150 people. I am deeply indebted to all of them, and particularly to those who put themselves at some professional risk by confiding in me. I also want to thank the public relations pros who facilitated many of the interviews and were subjected for their trouble to my ludicrous demands and last-minute changes of schedule: at the DOJ, Michael Gordon and Gina Talamona; at Netscape, Chris Holten and Suzanne Anthony; at Intel, Pam Pollace and Tom Waldrop; at Sun, Susanne Vagadori, Anne Little, and Lisa Poulson; at Novell, Raymond Nasr; at AOL, Kathy Bushkin; and many others in Washington, DC, and Silicon Valley.

Microsoft deserves a mention apart from the rest. Without the company's cooperation, this book might still have been possible, but it would have been far poorer. In arranging interviews for me with most (though not all) of the executives I wanted to see, and especially in granting me not one but two audiences with Gates, Microsoft was taking a calculated gamble. I suspect its PR specialists are unlikely to feel the wager paid off, but I hope they regard the book as fair, even-handed, and accurate. In particular, I owe debts to Vivek Varma, who worked hard on my behalf during the summer of 2000, especially in securing my final meeting with Gates; to Mark Murray, who was a rich source of insight into the trial; to Mich Mathews, who over the years has never been anything but professional and good humored; and to Marianne Allison and her colleagues at Waggener Edstrom, not least Sue Barnes and Suzanne Dennehy, who were as pleasant and helpful a pair of minders as any journalist could hope for.

There is one person without whom this book—not to mention the retention of some semblance of my sanity—would never have happened: Katrina Heron, the editor in chief of *Wired*. Katrina and I have been working together for five years now, and in that time she has proven to be not simply the best editor I have ever encountered but also the truest and most trusted of friends. In the spring of 2000, she lifted me out of a deep dark hole and set me to work on a long article about the trial for *Wired*—a cover story eventually headlined "The Truth, the Whole Truth, and Nothing but the Truth," which ran to nearly 50,000 words and became the basis for *Pride Before the Fall*.

Acknowledgments

Katrina's imagination and commitment to the Microsoft story were rare and magnificent, and they were matched by those of her incredible editorial team at *Wired*, whose patience and fortitude I repeatedly pushed past the breaking point. Kristine Kern endured my flagrant disregard for deadlines with nary a peep of complaint. Daniel Carter designed a spectacular cover and came up with a layout that somehow made the most text-heavy of stories seem crisp and light. Christa Aboitiz ginned up a fantastic set of photos on a moment's notice and then commissioned an oil painting of Gates that captured the article's themes in a single elegiac image. Bill Goggins stayed up all night (more than once) and saved me from myself (more than once). Evan Ratliff fact-checked both the article and the book; all errors in either incarnation I lay squarely at his feet. Robert Pini and Maurie Perl saw to it that the article received more than its share of attention in the media. Other *Wired* ones to whom I owe thanks include Alex Heard, Emily McManus, Van Burnham, Jennifer Hillner, Valerie Hamilton, Chip Bayers, Martha Baer, Susana Rodriguez De Tembleque, Federico Gutierrez-Schott, Zana Woods, Carloyn Rauch, Melanie Cornwell, Julie Rose, and Rebecca Smith Hurd.

I am immensely grateful to my agent, Andrew Wylie, and his protégé, Jeff Posternak, who saw in the *Wired* piece the basis for a book. At HarperCollins, Adrian Zackheim skillfully—and quickly—shepherded the project to its completion. I owe a round of applause also to the members of his team—especially Joe Veltre, Sarah Beam, Charlie Schiff, Diane Aronson, Leah Carlson-Stanisic, and William Ruoto.

In the past three years, I have been supported by three research assistants: Leslie Albrecht, Polly Sprenger, and Chris Gaither. Each labored tirelessly, to terrific effect. Also terrific has been Bonnie Steiger, the world's greatest living microcassette transcriber. Throughout the trial, Elizabeth Shogren gave me a place to stay in Washington, not to mention unfailing and unqualified support. John Battelle provided me an office in San Francisco, asking nothing in return but the occasional (well, more than occasional) bourbon; his team at *The Industry Standard* made me feel at home and refrained from asking (much) what the hell I was doing there. Kenny Miller, Rachel Leventhal, and my incomparable goddaughter Zoe made New York feel like a second home, as did Mike Elliott, Emma Oxford, and their absurdly precocious daughters Roxana and Gina. James Bennet, Kate Boo, Denise Caruso, Lisa Clements, David Dreyer, Mary Ellen Glynn, George Hodgman, Jon Katz, Kerry Luft, Sebastian Mallaby, John Micklethwait, Oliver Morton, Neil Parker, Katherine Petrin, Carl Steadman, and Will Wade-Gery all provided moral or editorial support at one or another critical juncture.

Finally, what I owe Elise O'Shaughnessy for her labors makes the Third World's debt seem like pocket change. Elise listened to me talk (and talk) the story through on the phone. She read and helped edit the early drafts; she copyedited and proofread the later ones. She bucked me up ceaselessly and nagged me ruthlessly. She even came up with the book's splendid title. God only knows why she did all she did. And God only knows where I'd be if she hadn't.

John Heilemann
San Francisco, California
November 2000

For a complete index to *Pride Before the Fall*,
please visit the official Web site:

www.pridebeforethefall.com